THE BIG BOOK OF **WEATHER**

THE BIG BOOK OF WEATHER

A LOOK AT HOW THINGS WORK FOR KIDS

Jessica Stoller-Conrad

ROCKRIDGE PRESS

*For Tim, Freddie, and Felix, who bring sunshine
on even the cloudiest of days.*

Interior and Cover Designer: Brian Lewis
Art Producer: Meg Baggot
Editor: Jed Bickman
Production Editor: Ashley Polikoff

Illustrations © 2020 Stuart Holmes; Character Illustrations by Emily Emerson; Cover Photography, Science Source: NASA/NOAA, Mike Hollingshead, James Steinberg, NOAA, Dean Muz/Design Pics, K. Kent/Storm, William D. Bachman. Interior photography, ScienceSource: Kenneth Libbrecht (x), Gregory K. Scott (26), Art Wolfe (27), Georg Gerster (28), Jon G. Fuller/VWPics (29), Michael S. Nolan (57), Dr Juerg Alean (58), Martin Rietze (58), Mark Newman (141); Alamy: Science History Images (81), NSF (81), Signal Photos (81), Vicki Beaver (131); Shutterstock: (10, 31, 59).

Author photo courtesy of Chelsea Mason.

ISBN: Print 978-1-64611-396-5 | eBook 978-1-64611-397-2
R0

CONTENTS

Introduction vi

PART ONE Weather Basics 1

    Chapter 1: Can You Really Control the Weather? 1

    Chapter 2: What Is a Weather Phenomenon? 7

PART TWO Just Your Basic Weather Phenomena 13

    Chapter 3: Wind 13

    Chapter 4: Clouds 25

    Chapter 5: Rain 43

    Chapter 6: Snow 55

    Chapter 7: Fog 67

    Chapter 8: Dust Storms 79

PART THREE Natural Disasters: We're Not in Kansas Anymore 91

    Chapter 9: Tornadoes 93

    Chapter 10: Hurricanes 105

    Chapter 11: Wildfires 117

    Chapter 12: Ice Storms 129

    Chapter 13: Weather or Not? 141

Glossary 145

Resources 149

Experiment Index 151

Index 152

Introduction

What in the World?

You're enjoying a beautiful, sunny morning at the beach, but by noon it turns into a windy, rainy mess. Or you feel perfectly comfortable wearing a T-shirt and shorts to school one day—but just a week later, you find yourself shivering in a heavy coat. Dealing with our planet's weather can be tricky.

What in the world is going on? Well, even if it often seems that the weather just changes randomly, there *are* actually scientific reasons for all those crummy beach days and surprise cold snaps. And in this book, you'll learn everything you could want to know about these kinds of wacky changes and other weather events that you see and hear about every day. When you've finished the book, you'll know a lot more about how weather and climates work.

But First, a Little About Me

Like you, I've always wondered why the world works the way it does. Growing up in northern Indiana, I had a chance to experience the extremes of all four seasons every year, which led this curious kid to ask lots of questions.

For example, there were thunderstorms all the time in the summer, but we only got warnings of tornado dangers every once in a while. So I'd wonder: What's the difference between a regular old thunderstorm and one that makes tornadoes? In the winter, we'd get loads of snow, but I noticed it wasn't always the right kind of snow to be packed and shaped into a snowman or a snow fort. And I'd ask: Why can some snow be packed into a ball, but other snow just flakes apart?

As I got older, I remained fascinated with learning and asking questions. I learned that scientists spend a lot of time looking at the world and asking why things are the way they are, so I decided that I wanted to become a scientist.

I became a biologist—a scientist who studies life—and I made observations, asked questions, designed experiments, and even discovered things. It was wonderful. But eventually I realized that what I loved most of all was *telling* friends and family about what I'd learned and getting them excited about science, too.

That's why I became a science writer—a person who explains what science has taught us about how the world works—and that's why I'm so excited to teach you about the science of weather in your world!

What You'll Find Here

This book contains dozens of easy-to-understand explanations of weather events, sometimes called **weather phenomena**. (A single event is a **phenomenon**. If those words look unfamiliar to you, it's because they come from the language of the ancient Greeks.)

> Psst . . . You'll see **boldface** words peppered throughout the book. These are terms that are important for budding scientists to understand. You'll always find a definition near the word in bold, and all of the important terms are listed with their definitions in the glossary at the back of this book.

But then we'll go one exciting step further. You're an important part of this book. You won't just read about a phenomenon, such as how clouds form; you'll use the experiments I've included to see for yourself how and why it happens. Using a few simple ingredients, you'll be able to watch clouds form in your very own kitchen!

Why are these experiments important? Well, first of all, they're fun! You'll get to make things that steam and bubble and do all sorts of wild stuff. But it's not just fooling around. The experiments in each chapter are designed to help you learn about all the concepts you've just read about. There is no better way to learn science than to do it yourself!

The Scientific Method

The experiments in this book are set up so that you can approach questions the way a real scientist would: using the **scientific method**. The scientific method is a process—a set of steps—that scientists follow when they try to answer questions about things we don't yet understand.

> **A true experiment always involves one or more questions. If you know exactly what will happen, it's just a demonstration.**

Here is how it works:

1. Record your observations about a topic you're interested in.

2. Think of a question you want to answer about this topic.

3. Form a hypothesis. A **hypothesis** is a possible answer to your question—what you think will happen. (The plural is **hypotheses**.) It has to be an idea you can test.

4. Design an experiment to test whether your hypothesis is true.·

5. Make a prediction about the outcome of your experiment.

6. Do the experiment and see what happens!

7. Think about whether the results of the experiment were the same as your prediction. How do the results help you answer your question and test your hypothesis? What did you learn?

I've helped you out by designing these experiments as a starting point, but you'll still be forming hypotheses and making predictions on your own. After you finish each experiment, you'll have to ask yourself a few more questions to get to the bottom of what's going on: Was your prediction correct? Did the results of the experiment support your hypothesis? What conclusions can you draw now that you've seen this phenomenon play out in real life?

What Will You Need to Get Started?

You probably don't have a full laboratory in the corner of your bedroom. So our experiments involve no special equipment like microscopes and no materials that are expensive or hard to find. Almost all the supplies you'll need to make the magic happen are things you probably already have around the house, and you should be able to find the rest at a grocery or craft store. My step-by-step instructions will make it easy for you—and sometimes a grown-up lab partner—to follow along.

Since weather and earth science are topics that you're probably already learning about in school, this book isn't going to repeat standard lessons about weather. Instead, it will provide extra explanations and useful bonus activities to take your learning even further.

Weather Skills Are Life Skills!

After you've experimented your way through this book, you'll have an impressive amount of weather knowledge to show off in science class. But learning about weather will help you outside of school, too. Knowing the factors that shape our weather can help you make outdoor plans—and help you stay safe as well. What you learn will also help you understand discussions about climate change and how it will affect our lives.

For example, what does it mean when your local weather forecaster says that a low-pressure zone is moving into your area? And how should that affect your plans to have your birthday party at the park in a few days?

You'll find the answers to these questions and more in these pages. So let's get ready to dig in!

PART ONE

WEATHER BASICS

CHAPTER 1

Can You Really Control the Weather?

Have you ever wondered why it rains? Or whether it's *really* true that no two snowflakes are exactly alike? Or what causes a hurricane to form? You're in luck, because in this book you can find answers to all of these questions—and more!

Each chapter of this book focuses on a different type of weather event, or phenomenon. (Some of you will want to go straight through from beginning to end. But if you want to investigate a particular weather topic, use the table of contents or the index to find it, and flip to that page.) Every chapter will start with easy-to-understand explanations of the science behind the weather phenomena you see and hear about every day. You'll also learn about how these weather events may change over time and what changes scientists think you're likely to see in your lifetime.

Because I know you're a proper scientist, I figured you'll want to do more than just read about the weather. So I've pulled together three different kinds of experiments to help you re-create the science of each weather event.

Quick Query: These simple activities will help you learn the science behind a weather event in just a few minutes.

Observation Deck: These experiments explore the concept a bit more deeply. You may need to wait a few hours or days to see results.

Take It Outside: We'll make nature our laboratory by using the actual weather happening outside to learn something new. (Some of these experiments may not cooperate with your local climate or the current weather. But don't worry; you'll have plenty of other experiments to choose from!)

I'll be guiding you to approach the experiments the way any real scientist would, by using the **scientific method**. Let's walk through an example of what that process looks like in real life.

It All Starts with a Hypothesis

You're walking outside, and you see a sky full of clouds. You wonder: How do clouds form?

If you flip to chapter 4 (page 25), you'll find some great information about clouds, what causes them, and how they are affected by climate change. Then you'll move on to the experiments.

Each experiment will start with a section called "The Big Idea," which will give you a bit of information about what you'll be doing and what the experiment will demonstrate. For example, in the "Clouds in the Kitchen" experiment on page 33, that section explains that you'll be re-creating the formation of clouds indoors with hot water, hair spray, a jar, and some ice cubes.

After you read through "The Big Idea" section, take a minute to think about what you've learned already in that chapter about how clouds form in nature. Think about what you're going to do in the experiment and how it relates to cloud formation. Form a hypothesis: What do *you* think will happen when steam from hot water is trapped in a jar with an ice-cold lid?

Before you dig into the experiment, grab a notebook and record your hypothesis. It might help to write this prediction as an if/then statement.

For example, you might predict: "*If* I trap the hot water vapor in the jar with a cold lid, *then* the water vapor will condense inside the jar to form a cloud."

Woo-hoo! We've just formed our first hypothesis together!

You're probably impatient to get to work on the experiment, but first you should carefully go over the "Cautions" section. This section will warn you if you need to use special equipment—or a grown-up lab partner—to help you stay safe during the experiment.

> **The "Cautions" section will help you stay safe during the experiment. It will warn you if any of the materials can be dangerous and if you need special equipment or a grown-up lab partner.**

Grab your rain boots and sunscreen, and let's go . . .

Test Your Ideas!

Before you dig into an experiment, read through the list of materials and make sure you have everything. You can probably find most of the things you need around the house. Any other required supplies should be easy (and inexpensive) to find at a grocery store, garden center, or craft store.

When you've made sure you're all ready, follow the step-by-step instructions I've provided.

Always remember: An experiment may not work exactly the way you expected the first time you try it, but that's okay! Troubleshooting, testing, and retesting experiments are all part of being a scientist. As a classmate once told me: "Research involves trying an experiment over and over again. If you only had to do it once, it would just be called 'search'!"

After you've followed the instructions and observed the result, read the questions in the "Observations" section and think about your answers. Did the results of the experiment match your prediction? If not, why not?

Don't be discouraged if the experiment shows that your hypothesis was wrong. Learning that something *isn't* true is just as important to science as learning what *is* true.

It's totally okay if you're feeling a little stumped. Experiments can sometimes seem like magic tricks, but there's no magic here—just science! You can find explanations of what happened and why in "The Hows and Whys" section that comes after the experiment. And if you encounter any new words in the explanations, you can always look them up in the glossary in the back of the book.

After you've gone through the experiment once, you might wonder: What would happen if I did it another way? If that's the case, check out the "Kick It Up a Notch!" section. I'll give you a few ideas about how to change up the experiment to try out other possibilities. These are just jumping-off points for your imagination; you should feel free to come up with your own modifications as well.

Never forget the most important step of any experiment: Have fun! There's no need to get it all right and learn everything there is to know on the first try. Just go outside, get a little messy, and have a great time.

CHAPTER 2

What Is a Weather Phenomenon?

A weather phenomenon is a natural event that is caused by a specific interaction among water, the **atmosphere**—the layers of gases and particles that surround our planet—and the land. Is it cloudy? Windy? Rainy? These are all examples of weather phenomena.

We mostly talk about the weather when it's unpleasant or ruins our plans, or sometimes when we see news about a natural disaster, such as a hurricane or tornado. But even when we're not thinking about it, weather is always happening all around us.

When it comes to weather, there is no such thing as an ordinary day. Even when it's mild outside and you don't notice anything remarkable, the oceans and the atmosphere are full of activity you can't see with just your eyes. This activity is the source of our weather!

There may be no ordinary weather days, but in every region there are *typical* weather days in each season of the year. For example, if you live in Michigan, a typical winter day might mean freezing temperatures and storms with snow and ice. If you live in Florida, though, a winter day is likely to be much warmer and milder.

As our planet continues getting warmer, the typical day in any region may change. A typical winter day in Michigan or Florida 30 years from now will probably be different from today.

No matter where you are, the atmosphere miles above you is constantly changing, and it can quickly change the weather along with it.

YOUR FRIENDLY NEIGHBORHOOD METEOROLOGIST

Meteorology is the field of science that involves studying our atmosphere, how it changes, and how it affects our weather. A person who studies meteorology is called a meteorologist.

If you've ever checked a weather forecast online or on TV, you've seen and used the work of meteorologists. These scientists collect and analyze information about the atmosphere and oceans to understand how changes in the water and sky will affect our weather.

How do they do this? Well, meteorologists are scientists, so they use the scientific method. That begins with making observations, and meteorologists do that in several ways. Of course they look outside to see what's happening in the sky right now, but that doesn't give them enough information to forecast what will happen with the weather. They use many tools to collect information—another way of making observations.

For example, meteorologists use information collected from **weather stations** to help make their forecasts. A weather station is made up of several types of instruments that are constantly collecting information about the weather in a specific area. Weather stations are set up in towns and cities all over the world to measure temperature, air pressure, wind speed, humidity, and rainfall.

But meteorologists don't just gather information from the ground. They also get clues from the sky using instruments on research airplanes and **weather satellites**. Weather satellites are machines that orbit high above Earth, collecting information about the temperature, gases, water vapor, and clouds in our atmosphere.

Together, all this information helps meteorologists figure out weather forecasts for your area. Weather forecasts from meteorologists can help you figure out if tomorrow is going to be a good day for a picnic or warn you that you'll need to seek safety during a major storm.

People often joke about how often weather forecasts are wrong. Actually, forecasting has become more and more accurate over the past 20 years. Most one- to three-day forecasts are good predictors of what to expect, and advance warnings of severe weather often help people save their property—and even their lives!

Unfortunately for meteorologists, people generally only notice and remember the times when they get it wrong.

There are so many factors that go into weather, and their interactions are so complex, that even the most powerful computers can't always predict it accurately. Forecasts are more reliable when they don't look too far into the future, but meteorologists will never be able to predict the weather with absolute certainty. So you should probably keep an umbrella handy no matter what the forecast says.

Weather, Climate, or Atmosphere?

Weather describes the conditions in Earth's atmosphere at a certain place and time. Weather is temporary—it changes all the time. Heat, rain, snow, and wind are all kinds of weather. And a sunny day can easily be followed by a rainy one.

Climate, on the other hand, describes the average weather conditions in a region over decades, centuries, or even longer. To describe a region's climate, we might say how hot or cold it is in different seasons, how humid or windy it is, or how much rain or snow usually falls.

Weather changes from day to day, or even hour to hour, but climate stays about the same from year to year. For example, much of Florida has a subtropical climate. There might be a cold day here and there, but on average, the weather will be warm and humid.

Weather and climate have one important thing in common: Earth's atmosphere. Changes in the weather are almost always a result of changes in the atmosphere. And changes in Earth's climate have to do with the atmosphere, too.

Weather is affected by the gas molecules that make up the air we breathe. The atmosphere is composed of nitrogen, oxygen, and small amounts of other gases. There are billions and billions of molecules of these gases in our atmosphere. Even though they are far too tiny for us to see, the weight of all of those molecules adds up. We refer to how heavily the air is pushing down toward Earth's surface as **air pressure**.

Because the molecules are not evenly distributed, there can be large differences in air pressure, which affect the weather. In areas of high pressure, the gas molecules in the atmosphere push down so strongly that clouds can't even form. High-pressure days are fair-weather days. In areas

continued →

of low pressure, the air isn't nearly as heavy. This means that clouds can form, bringing rain and snow with them.

Climate is also affected by Earth's atmosphere, but in a different way.

Have you ever seen a greenhouse? They are glass buildings that people can use to grow plants that need warmth without using a powered heater. The glass walls and roof allow the Sun's rays to shine in, but they keep the Sun's heat from leaving, making the inside of the greenhouse warmer.

Certain gases in our atmosphere also trap the Sun's heat. This phenomenon is called the **greenhouse effect**. Like the glass walls and roof of a greenhouse, **greenhouse gases** in our atmosphere allow the Sun's rays to shine in, then trap its heat inside, warming Earth's surface.

Earth needs greenhouse gases—they are essential to life! Without them, Earth would be too cold to live on, and crops would be unable to grow. However, we need the right balance of these gases in our atmosphere. Too many greenhouse gases would make Earth too hot to be comfortable for life.

Unfortunately, many human activities, such as burning gasoline in a car engine or coal in a power plant, increase the amount of greenhouse gases in our atmosphere. And these extra greenhouse gases are causing our planet to warm up more than it would naturally. This **global warming** can have very complicated effects.

As Earth warms, the atmosphere and oceans warm, too. Rising global average temperatures can cause complex changes in weather patterns across the planet. We call this **climate change**. For example, scientists predict that extreme weather—such as heat waves and large storms—will become more frequent or intense as these temperatures rise.

Although Earth's climate is already warming, there are things we can do to slow this human-caused change. Scientists are already working on this big problem—and you and I can do our part by learning more about Earth's atmosphere and how to keep it healthy.

PART TWO

JUST YOUR BASIC WEATHER PHENOMENA

CHAPTER 3

Wind

Have you ever felt a gentle breeze on your face? Or seen a pile of leaves drift down the street? Thanks to Earth's atmosphere, we're surrounded by air all the time. But you might not even notice that it's there if it weren't for wind.

In general, wind happens when warm air rises and cool air rushes in to replace it. So where's the best place to find wind? It's very common to see windy conditions on the coasts of large bodies of water, such as oceans and lakes. The warm afternoon sun heats up the air near the coast, causing it to rise. And when that happens, cool air from above the water blows in to replace it. These winds are called sea breezes and lake breezes.

Is there any place that doesn't have wind? For centuries, sailors have used the **trade winds**—winds that blow steadily in a curved pattern toward the equator—to travel the seas. But near the equator, where these winds from opposite directions meet, is an extremely calm region called the **Doldrums.** The Doldrums have so little wind that sailing ships can get stranded there for weeks at a time! (At some point, people started using "in the doldrums" to mean "feeling down or blue." That's probably how sailors stuck in the Doldrums felt!)

HOW DOES IT DO THAT?

As you've probably already gathered, **wind** is moving air. But you may not know that wind is caused by differences in air temperature and pressure. How does this work? Well, it all starts with the Sun.

Because of how Earth is tilted on its axis, the Sun heats Earth unevenly. This creates patches of warmer and cooler air in our atmosphere. In general, Earth is warmer near the equator and colder near the poles. But there are also many other regions of warm and cold air that are caused by lakes, mountains, valleys, and other features of the land and water.

Warm air is less dense, or heavy, than cool air, so it rises upward. As all these air molecules rise, that means they're no longer pushing down heavily on Earth's surface below. This creates an area of low air pressure beneath the patch of warm air. Air flows from areas of high pressure to areas of low pressure. So as warm air moves up, denser, cooler air rushes in to take its place. This movement of air creates wind.

Up, Up, and Away?

You've probably seen it in movies like *Up* . . . but is it really true? Could a house really be lifted up by a bunch of balloons? And how many balloons would it take?

The answer is a little complicated. After all, it depends on the size of balloons, the size of the house, and whether or not the house is fastened to a foundation in the ground. Regardless of the details, it would take *a lot* of balloons to lift a house. Technicians at Pixar were said to have estimated that in real life, it would take *23.5 million* helium balloons to lift the 1,800-square-foot house in the movie *Up*.

Although no one has tried this exact experiment, people have flown with helium balloons in real life many times. In fact, the activity even has a name: cluster ballooning.

In 2011, a group of scientists, engineers, and two balloon pilots built a small house—16 feet by 16 feet, about 1½ times the size of a parking space—and lifted it 10,000 feet in the air for over an hour. The experiment took a cluster of 300 helium-filled weather balloons that each measured about 8 feet in diameter. So flying a house is possible, but you probably shouldn't try it at home.

If wind is created when warm air at the equator rises up and cold air from the poles rushes in to fill the space, wouldn't all winds blow toward the equator? Not exactly.

First of all, geographic features like mountains and oceans can complicate the direction that the wind is blowing. Second, we need to remember that Earth is constantly spinning on its axis. (That's why we experience day and night!)

As wind above Earth's surface rushes from areas of high pressure to areas of low pressure, the planet underneath all that air is still rotating. This causes the winds above Earth's surface to change direction slightly. The rotating Earth makes winds in the Northern Hemisphere deflect toward the right, while winds in the Southern Hemisphere deflect toward the left. This interaction between the spinning Earth and the atmosphere is called the **Coriolis effect**.

Wind is generally described with a measure of speed and the direction the wind is coming *from*. So if someone tells you there is an east wind, that means there is a wind blowing from east to west. A west wind, on the other hand, blows from west to east.

The wind you're probably most familiar with is the wind you can see blowing in trees near the ground. These are called surface winds. But did you know that winds can be found much higher in the atmosphere, too? For example, five to nine miles above Earth's surface are **jet streams**: bands of strong winds that blow from west to east across the globe.

To the Extremes!

Antarctica is widely considered to be the windiest place on Earth. Although other places have occasionally had stronger wind gusts, the average maximum daily wind speed in Cape Denison, Antarctica, is 44 miles (71 kilometers) per hour—and gusts of wind can reach more than 200 miles per hour! Cape Denison is also very cold, with temperatures often reaching far below 0°F (–18°C) in the winter.

Can a human survive in this harsh environment? Yes! Researchers actually live in canvas tents at Cape Denison to perform studies. Although human researchers are usually only temporary visitors, many penguins make windy Cape Denison their permanent home.

Jet streams, which travel at more than 100 miles per hour, can transport storms and other weather systems across the country. They can even help an airplane travel from Los Angeles to New York in much less time than it takes to make the return trip.

As the warming Earth causes climate change, the jet streams are changing—which also changes the weather. The North and South Poles are warming faster than other regions on Earth. This means that the temperature differences between the poles and the equator are not as dramatic as they once were, leading to weaker jet streams.

Power On!

If you've ever gone on a road trip through the Great Plains in the United States, it's very likely you've seen giant windmills on the horizon. But how do those windmills turn a windy day into electricity that powers your lights, TV, and refrigerator?

The spinning parts of the windmill are called wind turbines. The blades on the turbines catch the wind, making the turbines spin. This spinning movement created by the wind then powers an electric generator that turns the energy from the spinning turbine into electricity.

Where are the best places to put a windmill? Some of the best places to find strong, regular winds are round hilltops, open plains, and gaps in mountains that can funnel the wind. The five US states that produce the most wind energy are Texas, Oklahoma, Iowa, Kansas, and California. In 2018, these states produced more than half of the wind energy harnessed in the United States!

Take Control/Get Involved!

Ready to get swept away? In the experiments up next, we'll learn about how wind is created, build a device to predict when big winds might be coming, and figure out what the wind in your area is carrying.

Earlier in this chapter, we learned about how wind is caused by warm air rising and cool air rushing in to take its place. In the first experiment, you'll use a few basic ingredients at your kitchen table to see how this works. Because it's hard to see the movement of air, we'll use smoke to track where the air is traveling.

Air pressure is also important in the formation of wind, as air moves from areas of high pressure to areas of low pressure. The second experiment here will teach you how to make a **barometer**—an instrument used to measure air pressure. You'll be able to use it to track changes in air pressure where you live. These readings can help you predict whether wind and storms might be on the way.

Finally, we'll go outside for the third wind experiment, where you'll learn exactly what is in the wind. Although the air we breathe is mostly made up of nitrogen, oxygen, and a few other gases, particles such as smoke, pollen, and dust are floating around in the atmosphere, too. In this experiment, you'll create a sticky trap to collect and analyze these particles—called **aerosols**—that are carried by the wind.

Now let's get ready to see air temperature, air pressure, and wind in action!

1. Up in Smoke!

Quick Query

The Big Idea: Wind starts with warm air rising into the atmosphere. In this experiment, you'll use smoke to track the movement of air between two jars of different temperatures. What do you think will happen when you place a jar of cool, dense air on top of a jar of warm and less dense smoky air?

CAUTIONS: Have an adult lab partner help you with using the matches and lighting the incense or mosquito repellent coil. Be careful to handle glass jars very gently so that they do not break.

Materials:

- 2 empty, narrow-mouth 1-quart jars
- Table
- Tape
- Black construction paper

- Matches
- Incense in pieces small enough to fit in the jars, or mosquito repellent coil
- 1 (3-by-5-inch) index card

The Steps:

1. Put one of your empty jars into the freezer.

2. Go outside and find a non-windy spot that will be a good place to do your experiment. You'll need a flat surface (like a table) with a wall behind it.

3. Tape a piece of black construction paper to the wall behind where you will do the experiment.

4. Get an adult to help you strike a match, then light the incense or mosquito coil according to the instructions on the packaging.

5. Turn the non-frozen jar upside down and place it over the burning incense. Watch the jar fill with smoke, which should take only a few minutes.

6. Turn the smoke-filled jar right-side up. As quickly as you can, put an index card over the mouth of the jar to cover it. Bring the covered jar to the table.

7. Go inside and get the frozen jar out of the freezer. Turn the frozen jar upside down and place it on top of the smoky jar. The index card should be between the two jars.

8. Lift the frozen top jar very slightly—just enough to wiggle out the index card. Immediately put the mouth of the frozen jar back on top of the mouth of the smoky jar.

9. Place your stacked jars on the table in front of the black construction paper on the wall. Observe what happens.

Observations: What happened to the warm, smoky air? Was the black construction paper helpful, and, if so, why?

Kick It Up a Notch: Try doing this experiment again, only with the smoky jar on top and the frozen jar on the bottom. How do you think the outcome might change?

The Hows and Whys: Air is made up of trillions of gas molecules. As air heats up, the gas molecules bounce around more quickly, trying to escape whatever contains them—in this case, the sides of the jar. Because of these bouncing molecules, the warm, smoky jar is an area of high air pressure. When air is cold, however, the gas molecules move more slowly and don't bounce off the sides of the jar very much. So the cold jar is an area of low air pressure. When you connected the jar openings, the air moved from the area of high pressure to the area of low pressure—just like pressure differences in our atmosphere create wind.

2. Pressure's On: Make Your Own Barometer

Observation Deck

The Big Idea: A drop in air pressure can mean a storm—and strong winds—are on the way. In this experiment, you'll make a barometer, which is an instrument used to detect local changes in the atmospheric pressure. If it's a nice day outside, what do you predict your barometer reading will be?

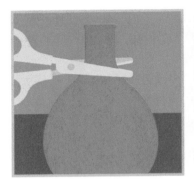  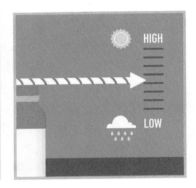

CAUTIONS: Have an adult lab partner help you with the superglue. Be careful to follow all directions on the package, and don't let the glue contact your skin.

Materials:

- Scissors
- Latex balloon
- 1-quart jar
- Rubber band
- Superglue

- Paper or plastic straw
- Arrow cut out of paper
- Paper or card stock
- Pen or pencil
- Tape

The Steps:

1. Find a good spot for your experiment. A table next to a wall will work nicely.

2. Use the scissors to snip the neck off the balloon. Cut it at the spot where the narrow neck meets the circular body of the balloon. Discard the neck of the balloon.

3. Stretch the remaining body of the balloon over the top of the 1-quart jar. Use the rubber band to secure the balloon around the mouth of the jar.

4. Put a dot of superglue on the end of the straw and place it so that the glued end is attached to the middle of the balloon. The other end of the straw should hang over the edge of the jar.

5. Insert the non-pointed end of the paper arrow into the hollow end of the straw that is hanging off the edge of the jar. The pointed end of the arrow will indicate the level of the atmospheric pressure.

6. Tape the piece of paper on the wall next to the table. Place your jar next to the paper and draw a line at the level where the pointer is. Draw a line slightly above the pointer and label it "high." Draw a line slightly below the pointer and label it "low."

7. Record the position of the pointer in the data table below once or twice a day. As you record the barometer reading, record what the weather is like as well. Look at a weather forecasting app or website and also record what weather is expected in the next 24 hours.

Observations: What was the weather like when your barometer showed low atmospheric pressure? What about when the atmospheric pressure was high?

Kick It Up a Notch: Want a more precise barometer reading? Instead of just marking "high" and "low" above and below the initial reading, assign a number scale to your barometer. For example, you could draw five lines labeled 1 through 5 above the pointer and five lines labeled –1 through –5 below the pointer.

The Hows and Whys: When the atmospheric pressure is high, the weight of the gases in the atmosphere pushes down on Earth's surface. So when there's high air pressure, the gases push down heavily on the center of the balloon, causing the pointer to move up. When the air pressure is low, the gases in the jar begin to drift up. This causes the center of the balloon to move up and the pointer to move down. Low pressure can mean rainy weather is on the way. High pressure is often associated with mild or cold weather.

	DAY 1	DAY 2	DAY 3	DAY 4	DAY 5
Air pressure: Morning					
Air pressure: Afternoon					

3. Particle Catchers

Take It Outside

The Big Idea: The wind blowing around outside is more than just air—lots of fine particles, called aerosols, are also carried by the wind. In this experiment, you'll make simple devices to catch and analyze particles blowing in the air around your neighborhood. You'll collect particles from several different spots. How do you think the particles collected from under a tree will be different from those collected from a spot near the street?

CAUTIONS: None! This activity is safe for all ages.

Materials:

- Tape
- 4 pieces of string, cut into 12-inch lengths
- 4 blank white index cards
- Pen
- Cotton swab
- Petroleum jelly
- Zippered sandwich bag
- Magnifying glass

The Steps:

1. Tape a piece of string to each of the index cards. The string will be used to hang the cards in different locations.

2. Label the four cards: "Indoors," "Yard," "Tree," and "Control."

3. Dip the cotton swab into the petroleum jelly. Use it to coat most of the surface of one side of each card with a thin layer of petroleum jelly.

4. Hang the "Indoors" card somewhere inside your house. Hang the "Yard" card in your yard (or any open grassy area) and the "Tree" card under the branches of a tree. Be sure to hang the cards in locations where they will be undisturbed for three days. Place the "Control" card inside the zippered sandwich bag.

5. After three days, go to each of your sampling locations and get your index cards. Use the magnifying glass to examine each card for aerosols that were caught in the petroleum jelly. Compare the cards to the "Control" card. Record your findings in the data table below.

Observations: Which card collected the most aerosols? What aerosols do you think were trapped in the petroleum jelly? What do you think are the sources of the particles you collected?

Kick It Up a Notch: Think of a few other locations where you might be able to sample. Could you collect a sample near a busy road? Or perhaps in different rooms of your house? How do you think those samples would differ?

The Hows and Whys: Aerosols are any tiny particles that become airborne in the wind. Some examples are dust, smoke, car exhaust or other pollution, pollen, and ash from volcanoes. Aerosols are more concentrated in the air near where they were formed; for example, you'd find more ash particles in the air near a volcano and fewer particles the farther away you travel. The wind can carry aerosols thousands of miles from the source where they were picked up. (Smoke from the 2020 wildfires in Australia was detected in countries thousands of miles away and eventually circled the planet.)

	CONTROL	INDOORS	YARD	TREE
Particle count: (none/low/medium/high)				

CHAPTER 4

Clouds

Cloud watching is one of the most basic ways that people can interpret the weather. For example, a big, puffy white cloud on a sunny summer day can be a beautiful sight, while a giant, dark gray thundercloud could send you running indoors. Have you experienced a really cloudy day—or seen a cloud that seemed to have a very funny or familiar shape?

Generally, clouds form when warm, moist air rises up, then cools in the colder and higher parts of the atmosphere. **Water vapor** is the gas form of water, but as it cools, the water vapor condenses—or turns into droplets of liquid water—in the air. These collections of suspended water droplets are clouds. In some climates and seasons, clouds can also sometimes be made up of ice crystals suspended in the sky.

Clouds can form almost anywhere on Earth and in any climate, so long as there is warm, moist air available. However, in extremely dry regions, such as deserts, clouds are scarce.

Clouds in nature can be quite stunning. Their appearance ranges from wispy and delicate to dark and ominous. They can even take on some pretty wild shapes! But did you know those clouds are actually telling us a lot about the weather?

Here are pictures of some of the most common cloud types and what they might tell us to expect in the weather forecast:

High Clouds (16,000 to 43,000 ft)

Cirrocumulus Clouds

Cirrus

These wispy clouds form high in the atmosphere—approximately three to seven miles above Earth's surface. A few cirrus clouds in the sky can be a sign that fair weather is here to stay for a while. But if there is a web of cirrus clouds in the sky, a warm front might be on its way, signaling a change in the weather.

Cirrocumulus

Cirrocumulus clouds look like long rows of tiny cotton balls all lined up together high in the sky. They usually mean that you can expect fair weather. If you live near the tropics, though, they might be a sign that a hurricane is on the way!

Cirrostratus

These are sheet-like clouds made of ice crystals that can spread out over the entire sky. They are so thin that you can often see the Sun or Moon through them. In the daytime, they make the sunshine look "milky." When you see cirrostratus clouds, it usually means a storm is coming soon.

Mid-Level Clouds (7,000 to 23,000 ft)

Altocumulus Clouds

Altocumulus

Fluffy gray and white altocumulus clouds form in groups in the atmosphere below the level where you find cirrus clouds. If you see them in the morning when you wake up, and it's warm and humid outside, you may see a thunderstorm in the afternoon.

Altostratus

These are blue-gray clouds that cover the whole sky, making the Sun or Moon appear a bit fuzzy. They mean that a storm with lots of continuous rain or snow could be on its way.

Low Clouds (Surface to 7,000 ft, though some can grow taller)

Cumulonimbus Cloud

Stratus

Stratus clouds make the sky appear gray and misty all over. They may look like a fog that hasn't quite reached Earth's surface. If you see them out the window, grab your umbrella: Drizzly weather usually accompanies these gray skies.

Nimbostratus

Gray, rough, gloomy nimbostratus clouds are located close to the ground. They sometimes cover the whole sky, and they almost always mean that continuous rain or snow is on the way.

Cumulus

These puffy, cottony clouds are what you usually think of when you imagine a cloud. They are gray and white and usually have a flat bottom. They don't give you a lot of hints about the weather; you can see them both in fair weather and before storms. But if the top of the clouds looks like a head of cauliflower, that could mean rain showers are coming.

Cumulonimbus

These clouds are enormous! They are puffy and gray and white, like cumulus clouds, but can grow miles into the atmosphere. They sometimes have flat tops and bottoms and can look a bit like anvils. Cumulonimbus clouds are usually bad news: They can bring rain, hail, lightning, or sometimes even tornadoes.

Unusual Clouds (not classified by height)

Lenticular Clouds

Lenticular

Lenticular clouds, which look a little bit like alien spacecraft, are formed when moving air hits a barrier such as a mountain range. These clouds don't tell us much about the weather, but they do look really cool.

HOW DOES IT DO THAT?

Clouds are some of the most beautiful things in nature. They look like puffy cotton balls or wispy feathers, but, amazingly, they're just made of air and water. How do they get up there? Evaporation!

The water in clouds starts out on Earth's surface, in oceans, lakes, and rivers. As this water is warmed by the Sun and blown in the wind, it begins to evaporate. **Evaporation** is the process by which a liquid turns into a gas: In this case, liquid water turns into the gas form of water—called water vapor.

Air high in the atmosphere is colder than air that is closer to Earth's surface. When water vapor in the air is warmed by the Sun, it rises up to this colder part of the atmosphere. The cool air there causes the water vapor to condense, turning it into liquid water droplets or ice crystals.

But to make a cloud, you need many, many water droplets. **Condensation** happens more easily and quickly if the water vapor has some kind of solid object to condense upon. A good example of this is the water you might see dripping down the outside of a cold soda can on a hot, humid summer day. There is a lot of water vapor in the humid air, but you can't see it until it encounters the surface of the soda can and appears as big drops of water.

There aren't any soda cans high in the atmosphere, but there are a lot of particles of dust and pollen. Water vapor can condense or freeze on these particles, creating tiny water droplets or ice crystals. When enough of these droplets or crystals form, you have a cloud!

The most common types of clouds, such as cumulus and cumulonimbus, form when warm, moist air rises and cools in the atmosphere. But clouds can form in other ways, too. Some result from a region's geography. For example, lenticular and stratus clouds form when wind blows into the side of a mountain or hill and pushes the air high up into the atmosphere. As this cool air rises, it forms clouds.

Clouds can also form when large masses of air meet each other at Earth's surface. These large masses of air are called fronts. Mid-level clouds (like altocumulus and altostratus) and high clouds (like cirrus, cirrocumulus, and cirrostratus) can form at **warm fronts**, where a warm mass of air slides on top of a cold air mass. Rain clouds (like nimbostratus and cumulonimbus) can also form at warm fronts.

A **cold front** occurs when a mass of cold air slides underneath a mass of warm air, thrusting the warm air higher into the atmosphere. Cumulus clouds often form this way, then grow into stormy cumulonimbus clouds. Other rain clouds can form at cold fronts, too.

Rain isn't the only thing clouds can bring—they also provide shade from the Sun. Clouds act like a giant umbrella high in the sky, blocking the Sun's rays and reflecting them back into space. So if a region is covered with clouds during the daytime, that area will be darker and a bit cooler than it would be on a sunny day.

Clouds don't always make the weather cooler, though. At night, clouds can actually help make a region warmer. During the day, the Sun's heat is transferred to soil and water on Earth's surface. After sunset, that heat begins to release back into the atmosphere. But if there are clouds in the night sky, they act like a blanket, trapping the stored heat closer to Earth's surface. This makes the area warmer than it would be without the clouds.

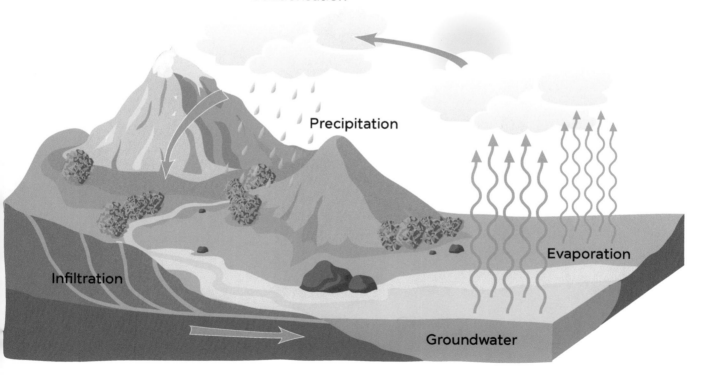

Condensation

Precipitation

Evaporation

Infiltration

Groundwater

To the Extremes!

Could you live somewhere that has an average of only about two hours of sunlight a day? That's exactly what it's like in Tórshavn, Faroe Islands—the cloudiest place on Earth. The Faroe Islands, which are part of the country of Denmark, are located about halfway between Norway and Iceland. Tórshavn, the capital city, is likely so cloudy because it is bordered by two mountains. If warm, moist air rises in the atmosphere, but it doesn't rise high enough to pass over a mountain, the air can get trapped, resulting in clouds and rain.

What is the least cloudy place on Earth? That award goes to the Atacama Desert in western South America. It has almost no clouds and hardly any rain at all. These cloud-free skies make the Atacama Desert a popular place for stargazing, and it's home to some of the world's most powerful telescopes. With no clouds to get in the way, nighttime in the Atacama offers spectacular views of our home galaxy, the Milky Way.

Take Control/Get Involved!

In the experiments in this chapter, you'll be making clouds, learning about how clouds affect temperature, and even trying to forecast your local weather based on the clouds! While you're doing these experiments, remember to think about the concepts we learned in this chapter, including condensation and cloud formation.

1. Clouds in the Kitchen

Quick Query

The Big Idea: In nature, clouds form when water droplets meet colder layers of the atmosphere high in the sky. But did you know that you can also make a cloud in a jar in your kitchen? It's true! In this experiment, you'll put boiling water and aerosol particles in the jar. What do you predict will happen when you use ice cubes to make the top of the jar very cold?

CAUTIONS: Have an adult lab partner help you with boiling the water. Be careful with the boiling water so that you don't get burned, and remember to handle glass jars very gently so they don't break. Be careful with the food coloring if you use it, as it can stain clothing and carpets.

Materials:

- 1 cup boiling water
- 1-pint glass jar with metal lid
- Food coloring (optional)
- Spoon (if you use food coloring)
- Hair spray
- Ice cubes

continued →

The Steps:

1. Have an adult help you pour one cup of boiling water into the 1-pint glass jar. If you're using food coloring, quickly add it to the water, and immediately stir it in with a spoon.

2. Quickly spray the hair spray into the jar and put the lid on top.

3. Put ice cubes on top of the metal lid of the jar.

4. Watch the air in the jar above the water and observe what happens.

Observations: What happened after you added ice to the lid of the jar? Is it what you expected to happen?

Kick It Up a Notch: Try doing the same experiment with jars of different sizes or with different amounts of boiling water inside the jars. How do you think the size of the jar and the amount of water will change what happens?

The Hows and Whys: In nature, warm, moist air rises up and cools as it gets to the higher, colder parts of the atmosphere. That's exactly what is happening in this experiment, too! What is the hair spray for? Remember: We learned that water droplets condense more quickly and easily if they have a solid object to condense upon. So the hair-spray particles floating around in the jar act just like the dust and pollen particles in our atmosphere. The warm, moist air in the jar rises up, is cooled by the cold air created by the ice, and then condenses on the particles of hair spray—creating your very own cloud!

2. Staying Cool Under a Cloud

The Big Idea: Clouds block heat from the Sun, so it's cooler on a cloudy day than on a sunny day. But how much cooler? In this experiment, you'll create sunny and cloudy days indoors, tracking just how much relief from the heat clouds can provide. How much cooler do you think it is when there are a few clouds in the sky during the day? And how do you think clouds affect the temperature at night, when there's no sunlight?

CAUTIONS: Ask an adult lab partner to help you with cutting the bottles and plugging the lamp into the wall. After the experiment is over, be sure to let the lamp cool down for at least 15 minutes before handling it. The heat bulb will make the lamp very hot. For best results, the heat bulb should be 60 to 75 watts, but be sure to choose a bulb and wattage that follows the lamp manufacturer's guidelines.

Materials:

- Desk-style lamp with heat bulb
- 2 clean, empty 2-liter plastic bottles with caps on
- Scissors
- 2 pieces of black construction paper
- Tape
- Cloud shapes cut out of aluminum foil
- 2 indoor or outdoor thermometers for measuring air temperature
- Pen or pencil
- Stopwatch

continued →

The Steps:

1. Put the heat lamp on a table near an electrical outlet. Do not turn the lamp on yet.

2. Take any labels off the plastic bottles, then use the scissors to cut them about one-third of the way down from the top. You'll use only the bottle tops in this experiment, so dispose of the rest of the plastic.

3. Cut the black construction paper into two circles just a little bigger around than the bottoms of the cut pieces of the bottles.

4. Tape the foil clouds to the front of one of the bottles.

5. Place the bottles side by side on the table, 6 to 8 inches in front of the heat-lamp bulb. Both bottles should be the same distance from the lamp, and the bulb should shine into the front of the bottles, not the top. Each bottle should get the same amount of heat. The cut-out clouds covering the front of one of the bottles should face the lamp, blocking some of the lamp's heat.

6. Place a black construction-paper circle under each bottle, with a thermometer lying on top of the circle. You should be able to read the temperature through the back of the bottles.

7. Record the starting temperature of each bottle in the data table on the next page at "0 minutes."

8. Start the stopwatch and turn on the lamp at the same time. Check the temperature every minute, and record that number in the data table. Do this every minute for 10 minutes.

Observations: Did the two bottles have different temperatures? If so, which one was warmer, and which one was cooler?

Kick It Up a Notch: Do the experiment again, but this time, try attaching clouds with different shapes to the cloud bottle. Observe whether this change makes any difference in the temperature. You can also try placing the clouds in different locations on the bottle. Do higher clouds block more light and heat than lower ones?

The Hows and Whys: You've probably noticed that a cloudy day is darker than a sunny one. But clouds block more than light—they block heat, too! During the daytime, clouds in our atmosphere reflect some of the Sun's light and heat back into space, helping us stay cool. In this experiment, the aluminum-foil clouds serve the same function. Because the foil clouds reflect the light and heat away from the bottle, they keep the environment cooler.

	CLOUD BOTTLE TEMPERATURE	CLEAR BOTTLE TEMPERATURE
0 minutes		
1 minute		
2 minutes		
3 minutes		
4 minutes		
5 minutes		
6 minutes		
7 minutes		
8 minutes		
9 minutes		
10 minutes		

3. Cloud Journaling

Take It Outside

The Big Idea: Can you predict the weather by reading the clouds? Find out by keeping a cloud journal for a week! Twice each day you'll go outside, look up at the sky, and record the types of clouds you see, as well as the temperature outside. You can use the cloud descriptions from earlier in this chapter to help you identify the clouds. The information I've provided about the different kinds of clouds will help you make a prediction about what kind of weather could be on the way. Will the cloud and temperature information help you make accurate predictions?

CAUTIONS: None! This activity is quite safe for all ages.

Materials:

- Cloud type descriptions from pages 26 to 29
- Outdoor thermometer
- Notebook (or use the data table on page 40)
- Pen or pencil

The Steps:

1. Pick a time in the morning and a time in the afternoon when you're able to observe and record the clouds. When the time comes, grab your cloud type descriptions, outdoor thermometer, notebook, and pen or pencil, then head outside.

2. In your notebook, write down the date and time. Use the thermometer to take an outdoor temperature reading, and record that in your notebook as well.

3. Next, find a comfy spot where you can sit down on the ground and look up at the sky. Use the cloud type descriptions to identify the clouds that you see, and record the cloud types in your notebook. Make any other notes you think will be helpful, such as the size or color of the clouds. Underneath your observations, write a weather prediction based on the clouds you saw. Rain? Snow? Clear skies?

4. Record the date, time, temperature, cloud types, and predictions twice a day for three to five days in your notebook or in the data table on the next page.

5. Each day, look back at the previous day's prediction. Put a checkmark next to the prediction if it was correct, and an X if it was wrong.

Observations: What kinds of clouds were the most common? Do you notice any relationship between the clouds you saw and the temperatures you recorded? Were you able to successfully predict any weather phenomena by looking at the clouds?

Kick It Up a Notch: Use the barometer you made in chapter 3 to record atmospheric pressure during each sampling period in addition to temperature and cloud types. See if you notice any relationships among air pressure, temperature, and cloud types.

The Hows and Whys: Clouds are more than just cool-looking puffballs in the sky—they tell us about the conditions in our atmosphere and what those conditions can mean for the weather ahead. Meteorologists look at clouds from the ground, from airplanes, and from orbiting satellites to help make their weather forecasts.

continued →

DATE AND TIME	OUTDOOR TEMPERATURE	CLOUDS OBSERVED	WEATHER PREDICTION
Day 1 morning			
Day 1 afternoon			
Day 2 morning			
Day 2 afternoon			
Day 3 morning			
Day 3 afternoon			
Day 4 morning			
Day 4 afternoon			
Day 5 morning			
Day 5 afternoon			

CHAPTER 5

Rain

Sprinkle. Spritz. Drizzle. Downpour. These are all names that we've given to the water that falls out of our sky—rain. Fresh water is necessary for life on Earth, and **precipitation**—such as rain—is one way we get it.

It can rain in almost any climate, all over the world. In order for rain to form, there needs to be moisture in the air and a temperature above freezing. That means that rain is very rare in dry climates—such as deserts—and cold climates—such as the Arctic and Antarctic.

HOW DOES IT DO THAT?

Rain obviously falls from the sky, but how did it get up there in the first place? And what made those drops eventually fall down to the ground?

The amount of water on Earth doesn't change much. We can't buy new water from another planet, but we can reuse Earth's water over and over again. And that's exactly what we do because of the **water cycle**. (See also page 31.)

The water cycle doesn't really have a beginning or end. Rather, it represents how water in (for example) the ocean becomes water in a cloud, which turns into water we can drink, which eventually ends up back in the ocean.

It all starts with the Sun. The Sun's heat warms water in the oceans, lakes, rivers, streams, and the soil. Some of that water evaporates, becoming water vapor in the air. Plants also release water vapor into the air. You've probably heard people talking about the amount of water vapor in the air by using the term **humidity**. On a humid day there is a lot of water vapor in the air.

After the water evaporates, air currents take the water vapor higher into the atmosphere, where it is cooler. The lower temperatures cause the water vapor to condense onto dust and other particles to form water droplets. These water droplets form clouds.

Water droplets in clouds combine to form bigger droplets. When they become too big and heavy to float in the air, these big water droplets fall to the ground as **precipitation**—rain, snow, sleet, or hail. As rain falls from clouds, most of it falls into the ocean or soil. People, animals, and plants all get the water they need to live from the soil or from bodies of water. That water eventually ends up back in the soil, ocean, or other bodies of water, and the process begins all over again.

Although water and sunshine are the key players here, wind is also an important part of the water cycle. If the world had no wind, water vapor would go straight up into the atmosphere, get cold, and come straight back down as rain. But that's not what happens. Air currents blow the clouds around in our atmosphere. This moves water droplets from place to place and keeps them suspended in the air for longer than they would be without wind.

What are some signals that rain is on the way? Well, as we discussed in the last chapter, certain types of clouds (such as nimbostratus and cumulonimbus) are a very good sign that rain is coming. A drop in air pressure can also be a sign that it is about to rain or that rain has just started.

Although rain is usually good news for people, plants, and animals, too much rain can be dangerous. For example, when a thunderstorm brings really heavy rain, sometimes there is a **flash flood**. In a flash flood, water rises so fast that people get caught off guard and homes and roads can flood.

Where do flash floods happen? It's possible to have one anywhere that rain comes fast and the water rises quickly. Yet certain areas are at higher risk than others.

Droughts

When a region gets a lot less rain than it normally would over a long period of time, we call it a **drought**. But "less rain than it normally would" can mean a lot of different things, depending on people's different situations. For example, a mayor might get concerned when a drought lasts for months, threatening her city's drinking-water supply. But even a couple of weeks without rain can ruin a farmer's crops if it happens at the wrong time.

A long stretch with no rain can cause soil to dry out and plants and animals to die. It can cause streams and rivers to shrink, or even dry up. Usually, rain fills lakes, ponds, and reservoirs with water that people can use in dry times. However, after too much time with little or no rain, this water either gets used up or evaporates. That's when water-supply problems begin, and that's often the beginning of a drought.

Although humans can't control when and how much rain falls from the sky, we can keep ourselves from running out of water, especially in dry years. The average American uses 80 to 100 gallons of water a day—for drinking, cooking, bathing, washing hands, and even flushing the toilet. That comes to more than 30,000 gallons every year. That's a *lot* of water!

We can use less water by following a few simple tips. For example, try to use water more than once. Did you give your dog a bath this weekend? Think about using eco-friendly pet shampoos so that you can use Sparky's bath water to water the plants! Do you have a big backyard? Think about replacing that water-guzzling grass with some native plants that are less thirsty.

To the Extremes!

If you're asked to name a rainy location, you might say "Seattle!" It does rain a lot in that city—about 150 days a year—but the amount of rainfall each day isn't that much. So Seattle ends up with a total of about three feet of rain in an average year, just a little more than the US average. But did you know there is a place that gets almost 13 times more rain than Seattle?

That place is the village of Mawsynram, in northeast India. On average, Mawsynram gets about a whopping 39 feet of rain each year. And most of that rain—90 percent of it—falls between May and October. This period is called monsoon season. (The word *monsoon* comes from an Arabic word meaning *season*.)

Why so much rain?

A **monsoon** happens when the Sun heats the ocean and the land unevenly in certain regions. In the summer, the land is usually warmer than the ocean. So all season long, moist air from the ocean blows onto the land and rises up in the atmosphere. For nearly six straight months, this phenomenon causes almost constant clouds, high winds, and heavy rain.

What's the driest place on Earth? Well, you already learned about this region in chapter 4: the Atacama Desert! Arica, Chile, in the Atacama Desert holds the world record for the longest recorded dry period. The city receives an average of only 0.03 inches of rain each year. In fact, Arica once had no rain at all for over 14 straight years!

As the global climate changes, deserts are changing, too. Some deserts are getting hotter, while others are actually getting wetter. Either way, the animals and plants that live in these environments are having to learn to either adapt or leave to survive. Not all of them will succeed.

For example, if an area has lots of plants and soil, most of the rainwater gets absorbed into the ground, so the area is less likely to flood. An area like a city or suburb, however, has lots of paved sidewalks and streets, which keep the water from going into the ground. This means that built-up areas are at higher risk for flash floods.

Climate change may have an effect on flooding, too. The warmer the air is, the more water vapor it can hold. As Earth's climate warms, the atmosphere will become able to hold more moisture. More moisture in the air means more precipitation—fueling more extreme weather events.

Take Control/Get Involved!

In the following experiments, you'll dig into how rain works and how it affects our environment. You'll learn how rain interacts with different types of soil, how the water cycle works, and how to figure out the amount of rain that fell during a storm. Let's get started!

1. Soil Soaker

Quick Query

The Big Idea: Have you ever wondered what causes a flood? Well, it's more than just a lot of rain! In this experiment, you'll test different types of soil to see which ones hold water and which ones let the water pass right on through. What soil material do you think will hold on to the most water?

  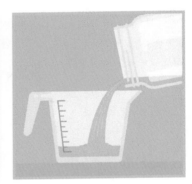

CAUTIONS: None! This activity should be safe for all ages.

Materials:

- Coffee filters
- Funnel
- Glass or plastic jar
- Pea gravel
- Liquid measuring cup
- Water
- Timer
- Sand
- Potting soil
- Powdered clay
- Pen or pencil

The Steps:

1. Put the coffee filter in the funnel, then place the funnel on top of the glass or plastic jar. The spout should point down into the jar.

2. Fill the coffee filter about ⅔ of the way up with pea gravel.

3. Use your measuring cup to measure 50 mL of water.

4. Set your timer for 2 minutes, but don't start it yet.

5. Pour the water over the pea gravel and immediately start your 2-minute timer.

6. At the end of the time, pour the water that has filtered into the jar back into your measuring cup. Record how much water got through.

7. Take the filter with the wet pea gravel out of the funnel. Replace it with a clean coffee filter, and fill the new filter ⅔ of the way up with sand, potting soil, or powdered clay.

8. Repeat the steps of the experiment until you have tested every material in the same manner. Always remember to record your results in the data table below—in this case, how much water filtered through each material.

Observations: Which substance held the most water? Why do you think that is?

Kick It Up a Notch: Try doing this experiment again with other materials. What is the soil in your neighborhood made up of? Try a scoop from your backyard in this experiment, and compare the amount of water to your earlier results. Is your soil more similar to sand or clay?

The Hows and Whys: Large particles—such as pea gravel—don't pack together as tightly as smaller particles. Water can filter through the spaces between the rocks and into the jar below. The same thing happens in nature. When rain falls on a rocky area of ground, the water can filter down through the rocks. But a tightly packed clay soil may be more prone to flooding.

MATERIAL	VOLUME OF FILTERED WATER
Pea gravel	
Sand	
Potting soil	
Powdered clay	

2. Water Cycle in a Bag

The Big Idea: The water cycle is essential to life on Earth. You wouldn't have water to drink or food to eat without it! In this experiment, you'll create your own tiny model of Earth, with a plastic sandwich bag acting as a stand-in for Earth's atmosphere. What do you think will happen when heat from the Sun reaches the water inside your bag?

CAUTIONS: This activity should be safe for all ages. But be careful with the food coloring if you use it, as it can stain clothing and carpets.

Materials:

- Liquid measuring cup
- Water
- Blue food coloring (optional)
- Permanent marker
- Zippered sandwich bag
- Tape

The Steps:

1. Measure out ¼ cup of water. If you are using blue food coloring, add it now. Set the water aside.

2. Use the marker to draw waves near the bottom of the zippered bag. Then draw a cloud and a sun near the top of the bag.

3. Open the bag and pour the water inside. Zip the bag closed. Make sure it's completely sealed.

4. Tape the bag filled with water to a window. Be sure to choose a window that will get sunlight.

5. Check on the bag each day for a few days until you notice changes. Be sure to record the changes you see.

Observations: What changes did you notice in the bag after a few days of heat from the Sun?

Kick It Up a Notch: Make several water cycles in bags. Tape one to each window in your house and see which window gives the best results.

The Hows and Whys: Heat from the Sun drives the water cycle on Earth, just as it does in this experiment. In the experiment, the sandwich bag acts like Earth's atmosphere, trapping the Sun's heat and Earth's moisture. The water at the bottom of the bag acts like the ocean, and as it heats, it turns into water vapor. At the top of the bag, the water vapor condenses into liquid droplets—a cloud.

3. Rain Tracker

Take It Outside

The Big Idea: Maybe you've heard a weather forecaster say that your area is expecting several inches of rain. In this experiment you can test those predictions by building your own rain gauge—a tool used to collect and measure rain. You'll build this tool and place it outside during a rainstorm, collecting the gauge after the storm to see how much rain fell. Build several gauges to test the rainfall in different spots—for example, under a tree or in a place where rain rolls off the roof of a house. Did the amount of rain in your gauges match your predictions?

CAUTIONS: Handle glass jars carefully so that they don't break.

Materials:

- Glass jars
- Funnels
- Permanent marker
- Ruler
- Duct tape
- Pen or pencil

The Steps:

1. Decide how many locations you'll need rain gauges for. Be sure to have that many jars and funnels.

2. Use a permanent marker and a ruler to mark and label the side of each jar every half inch for 5 inches. You'll do this by lining up the bottom of the ruler next to the bottom of the jar, then drawing a small line every half-inch. Label the lines "½ in," "1 in," "1½ in," "2 in," and so on, up to "5 in."

3. Place a funnel in the top of every jar. Use the duct tape to fasten each funnel securely to its jar. You don't want the rain to knock it off!

4. Now place your rain gauges in a variety of locations and wait for the rain to fall.

5. After it rains, collect your rain gauges and record how much rain is in each jar in the data table below, using the measurement markings on the sides of the jars.

Observations: How much rain did each gauge collect? Was it more or less than you were expecting? Did the location of the rain gauge make any difference?

Kick It Up a Notch: Compare your findings with the local weather report. If your results differed from the official record of the amount of rain for the day, try to figure out why.

The Hows and Whys: A rain gauge is an important tool in a meteorologist's toolbox. These readings are important, and not only because they tell us how much rain fell in a single storm. Tracking how much rain falls every year for many years also gives us information about an area's climate—and if it is changing to become, on average, wetter or drier.

RAIN GAUGE LOCATION	RAINFALL MEASUREMENT

CHAPTER 6

Snow

Have you ever lived in a climate that experiences snow? If you look up the weather report and see snow in the forecast, it can be kind of exciting. A blanket of snow can turn the world into a giant white sandbox. You can make castles and forts out of snow. If you live near a hill or mountain, you can go sledding or skiing. You can even have a snowball fight—one of the only times that it is 100 percent okay to throw a ball of frozen water at your friends and family members. You might even get a few days off school to enjoy all of this fun, too!

You might think that only very cold places have snow. That's partly true. To get snowy weather, a climate needs to have both moisture in the air and cold temperatures. That's why hot, dry deserts don't get snow very often.

However, the temperature down here on the ground doesn't have much to do with snow formation. Snow forms high up in the atmosphere when the temperature there is below freezing—less than 32°F (0°C). After the snowflakes form, they fall toward the ground. And if the temperature on the ground isn't too much warmer than freezing, you could be in for a snow day—woo-hoo!

HOW DOES IT DO THAT?

In chapter 5, we learned that rain forms when warm, moist air rises up into the higher, colder parts of the atmosphere and forms a cloud. The same is true for snow. So what happens differently to cause the cloud to form snow instead of rain?

In the formation of snow, warm, moist air rises up into very cold air that is near or below the freezing temperature. This is important. If the air is warmer than about 41°F (5°C), the precipitation will fall as rain or sleet, not snow. (It can be too warm to snow, but it can never be too cold to snow.)

The water vapor freezes into ice crystals instead of turning into water droplets. However, these ice crystals are very small—not the big fluffy snowflakes you're used to seeing.

Something else happens as the ice crystals form and begin to fall toward Earth. As they drift down, they travel through the warmer, moist air that is rising up. If the moist air is slightly warmer than freezing, it will melt the edges of the ice crystals. These melted edges cause the ice crystals to stick together and start to become snowflakes. When enough ice crystals stick together, they become too heavy to float and fall to the ground as snow.

Snowflakes that are created in an environment with lots of warm, moist air are very wet and sticky. This process is what forms the biggest snowflakes. Because of its stickiness, this kind of snow is also the best material for a snowman, a snow fort, or a snowball fight.

Snowman snow is called wet snow, but there is dry snow, too. If you've ever talked to someone who enjoys skiing, you've probably heard them talk about how they love hitting the slopes when there is "fresh powder." This kind of dry, powdery snow forms when smaller snowflakes fall down through cold, dry air. The edges of the snowflakes never get a chance to melt, so they don't stick together.

Dry snow isn't great for building snowmen, and it isn't great for driving on roads, either. Because the flakes don't stick together, dry snow can be easily blown across roads into big piles of snow called snowdrifts. If there is a lot of snow and the wind is strong enough, snowdrifts can be dangerous, blocking roads and even the doors of houses.

Strike a Pose

Individual snowflakes can be beautiful, but millions of snowflakes together can make beautiful formations, too! Here are a few snow art shows brought to you by nature:

Glaciers

Glaciers are made up of snow that has piled up over many years. Each layer of snow is pressed down by the weight of the snow that falls on top of it. The snow is pressed down so much that eventually it becomes ice—a glacier.

Snow is white, so why are many glaciers blue? As the snow is compressed, the structure of the ice changes. These changes cause the compressed ice to scatter and reflect blue light.

As Earth's climate changes, many glaciers around the world are shrinking.

Glaciers

Snow Cornice

A **snow cornice** forms when snow is blown by the wind at the sharp edge of a ridge or cliff face. The wind creates a ledge of snow and ice that overhangs the top of the cliff.

Be careful if you see a snow cornice! The ledge of snow it creates can fall off the cliff's edge. This is a risk for **avalanches**, masses of snow that slide down mountains.

*Snow
Cornice*

Snow Penitents

Snow penitents are spikes of snow that are compacted by certain patterns of melting and evaporation. They form most commonly in mountains, especially in the Andes Mountains along the west coast of South America. The pointy tops of penitents point toward the location of the noon sun, and they usually form in rows going east to west.

*Snow
Pentinents*

To the Extremes!

Imagine that you're riding a bus, and as you look out the window, all you can see is white snow. Above you, below you, beside you—snow is *everywhere*. Well, that's just what life is like in the mountains of the Japanese Alps on the island of Honshu. This area has the deepest snow in the world—or at least, in the parts of the world where people live.

A highway that goes through a snowy canyon in these mountains stays open to traffic all year long. The walls of snow that line the road can be 66 feet high, which is as tall as a seven-story building! If you ride in a bus or a car on this road in the middle of winter, it will feel like you are driving through a never-ending tunnel of snow.

Is there a place on Earth where it never snows? Absolutely! It has never snowed in the very warm climates of Guam, in the Pacific Ocean, and the US Virgin Islands, in the Caribbean Sea. Both of these islands have high temperatures all year round. The coolest they get is about 50°F (10°C), so it's never cold enough for snow to form.

Another place where it never snows may surprise you: the Dry Valleys of Antarctica. Although it's certainly cold enough for snow in the Antarctic, the air in the Dry Valleys region is some of the driest in the world. In fact, scientists think there hasn't been any rain or snow here in two million years!

Take Control/Get Involved!

Now that you've learned how snow forms in the atmosphere and how it ends up down on the ground, let's see some of this science in action! In these experiments, you'll learn how frost forms on a car windshield in the middle of winter, how routine ice crystals form into delicate snowflakes, and how much water is really in snow. Make sure you've got your hats and mittens, because this will be a chilly one!

1. Frost in a Can

Quick Query

The Big Idea: Have you ever noticed frost on a car windshield on a cold morning? Frost forms at cold temperatures when condensation—water vapor that becomes liquid water on a surface—freezes instead of remaining liquid. In this experiment, you will create your own frost by using cans, ice, and salt. What do you think will happen when you add ice to the cans? What do you think will change when you add the salt?

CAUTIONS: Be careful of any sharp edges on the opening of the metal cans.

Materials:

- Crushed ice
- 2 empty, clean metal cans (like those from canned soup)
- Salt

The Steps:

1. Add crushed ice to both metal cans.

2. Sprinkle salt on top of the ice in one can. The other can should have just ice inside.

3. Wait about 5 minutes.

4. Check the cans again. You should notice that frost has formed on the outside of one of the cans.

Observations: Why do you think the frost formed on the outside of that can? What do you think the purpose of the salt was?

Kick It Up a Notch: Try doing this experiment again by sprinkling other substances on top of the ice. Would sugar or baking soda have the same effect as salt? Why or why not?

The Hows and Whys: Have you ever seen someone pouring salt on sidewalks or roads after it snows? This is done because salt lowers the melting point of ice. So when you add salt to an icy sidewalk, the ice will melt even if the temperature outside is still below freezing. This helps prevent slippery roads and sidewalks. We used the same property of salt here! When we sprinkled salt on the ice, it lowered the melting point of the ice in the can. This made the ice melt very quickly—while the water vapor around the can dropped to temperatures slightly below freezing. The frost formed when the water vapor on the outside of the can froze.

2. Snowflake Factory

Observation Deck

The Big Idea: How are snowflakes made and why are they so light and fluffy? Find out in this experiment, in which you'll be making your own snowflakes! You'll be using dry ice (which you can get at most grocery stores), water, fishing line, and a few other simple supplies to create a small version of the atmospheric conditions that cause snowflakes to form. Are there some parts of the bottle that are warmer or colder than others? How do you think that will change the shapes of the snowflakes?

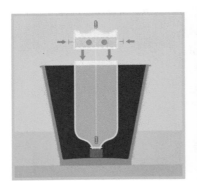 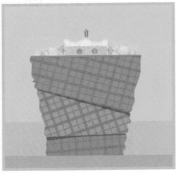 

CAUTIONS: Use care when handling dry ice, and have a grown-up lab partner help. Be sure to wear cloth or leather gloves, and use tongs or a spoon to move the dry ice. *Never* let dry ice directly touch your skin.

Materials:

- Scissors
- Clean, empty 2-liter plastic bottle with cap
- Sponge
- Safety pins
- Fishing line
- Sewing needle
- 2 paper clips
- Cloth or leather gloves for handling dry ice
- Dry ice
- Bucket
- Dish towels or rags
- Water
- Tape
- Magnifying glass

The Steps:

1. Use the scissors to cut off the bottom of the bottle at about 1.5 inches from the bottom. Set the top of the bottle aside for now.

2. Use the scissors to cut the sponge into a size and shape that will fit completely in the bottle bottom. Poke safety pins through the sides of the bottle bottom to secure the sponge inside it.

3. Cut a piece of fishing line about 10 inches long. Thread the fishing line through the eye of the needle, and tie a paper clip to the other end of the line.

4. Poke the needle up through the bottom of the bottle and then through the sponge inside. Pull the fishing line all the way through, until the paper clip on the end catches the bottom of the bottle. Take the needle off the fishing line and tie the other paper clip to that end of the line.

5. Wearing gloves, pour some dry ice into the bucket. Put the closed bottle top, with the capped-end down, into the dry ice in the bucket. Add more dry ice around the bottle, then wrap dish towels or rags around the bucket for insulation.

6. Wet the sponge that's in the bottle bottom, then tape the two pieces of the bottle back together. The bottle will be upside-down. Make sure the bottle bottom and sponge are not down in the dry ice.

7. You should begin to see crystals forming on the fishing line after 5 to 10 minutes. Use the magnifying glass to examine them up close. Within an hour, there should be plenty of snowflake-like ice crystals on the line.

Observations: What did the snow crystals look like? Were there different kinds? Did the crystals near the bottom of the fishing line look different from the ones near the top?

Kick It Up a Notch: Try wetting the sponge with warm water, room-temperature water, and very cold water. Does that affect the kinds of ice crystals that form?

The Hows and Whys: The sponge end of the bottle is moist from the water and relatively warm—room temperature—while the cap end of the bottle is very cold from the dry ice. This is kind of an upside-down version of the atmospheric conditions that grow snow crystals. As the water evaporates from the sponge, it becomes water vapor, and that water vapor begins to freeze into crystals along the line. This is a little different from the way snow forms in nature—snowflakes form from frozen water droplets, not water vapor—but this experiment is pretty close. In the atmosphere, and in our experiment, variations in humidity and temperature change the shape and structure of snowflakes. So if you noticed that the ice crystals at the bottom of the line looked a little different from those at the top, that is why!

3. How Much Water Is in Snow?

Take It Outside

The Big Idea: Fallen snow is made of snowflakes and air—but exactly how much water is in snow? In this experiment, you'll get to see how much water is in a few inches of snow. How much water do you think will result when the snow melts?

CAUTIONS: Handle glass jars carefully so that they don't break.

Materials:

- Glass jar
- Snow
- Dry-erase marker
- Ruler
- Pen or pencil

The Steps:

1. Bring your glass jar outside on a snowy day. Fill the jar almost to the top with snow. Use the dry-erase marker to mark the level of the snow on the side of the jar. Measure the height of the snow with the ruler and record this number in the data table on the next page.

2. Bring the jar inside, then wait until all of the snow has melted.

3. After the snow has melted, use your dry-erase marker to mark the level of the water in the jar. Use a ruler to measure the height of the water, and record the value in the data table.

4. Divide the number of inches of snow you started with by the number of inches of water you ended up with. That's how much snow it took to make 1 inch of water.

Observations: Did the melted snow produce more or less water than you were expecting?

Kick It Up a Notch: Do this experiment several times over the course of the winter, and record your findings each time. Do some types of snow contain more water than others?

The Hows and Whys: When snowflakes fall, they don't pack together tightly, so there is a lot of air between them. For this reason, snow carries much less water than rain. Though a storm bringing 12 inches of rain could result in a flood, a storm bringing 12 inches of snow won't be nearly as wet—even after the snow melts.

INCHES OF SNOW	INCHES OF WATER	SNOW PER 1 INCH OF WATER (Inches Snow / Inches Water)

CHAPTER 7

Fog

You get up in the morning and look out your window . . . and you see almost nothing. The tree in your neighbor's yard isn't visible, and you can't see the mailbox at the curb. Are you still asleep? Nope! It's just a foggy morning!

Fog basically forms like a cloud that touches the ground. And as you might expect, walking or driving through this cloud can be tricky. When fog is dense, visibility—how far a person can see—is very low. That means that driving a car or travel of any kind can be dangerous. Have you ever had to travel in fog?

In general, fog can form in most places with moisture in the air and temperature differences between the atmosphere and Earth's surface.

HOW DOES IT DO THAT?

Fog looks like a cloud near the ground, and in fact that's almost exactly what it is. Clouds form when very humid air rises up into colder parts of the atmosphere, condensing and forming water droplets.

Just like a cloud, fog can form more quickly when there are particles in the air—such as dust, smoke, or pollution. Have you ever noticed that fog often forms in the air over the ocean? Water droplets can condense on salt particles in the air to form fog, too!

However, fog forms like an upside-down cloud. During the day, heat from the Sun warms the ground. However, at night the ground is cooler. As moist air approaches the cool ground, it begins to condense, forming water droplets—just like a cloud. This type of fog is called **radiation fog**.

A different kind of fog, called **advection fog**, forms when warm air meets a cool surface. You may see advection fog along the West Coast of the United States. Cold ocean currents keep the air above the water colder than the air above the land.

To the Extremes!

In most climates, we take for granted the fact that on a typical day, we can hop in a car or bus and get from point A to point B. A foggy day is only an occasional inconvenience. But that's not the case in the Grand Banks, just southeast of the island of Newfoundland in Canada.

With approximately 200 foggy days per year, the Grand Banks is one of the foggiest places in the whole world. Why is it so foggy? This region is where a cold ocean current from the north and a warm ocean current form the south meet. The mixture of these two currents causes a regular fog to form over the whole area.

If a constant layer of fog isn't your thing, you could always move to the desert in the Southwest region of the United States. This area—covering parts of Nevada, Utah, Arizona, and New Mexico—has only a few days of dense fog in an average year.

In pictures of regions with lots of mountains, you'll often notice fog filling the valleys between them. This **valley fog** commonly forms at night and in the early morning. At night, the cool ground high in the mountains causes fog to form. But this dense, foggy air is heavy, so it slowly slides down the slope of the mountains and into the valleys below.

There are other ways fog can form, too. For example, **steam fog** forms over the tops of lakes, usually in the fall and winter. How? If a mass of cold air is on top of a mass of warm air near a lake's surface, this can lead to the rising warm air pushing the cold air upward. As the warm air lifts the cool air, the two air masses mix. This cools down the moist air right above the lake's surface, causing a steamy fog to form. This fog can look like vertical wisps rising from a lake.

When it's below freezing, the water droplets in a fog can freeze onto surfaces such as signs, car windshields, and roads. This can make for slippery driving conditions.

If the temperature becomes colder than 14°F (–10°C), **ice fog** can form. Instead of water vapor turning into water droplets, extremely cold air temperatures can turn water vapor directly into small ice crystals. This type of fog is most common in cold places such as Alaska and the North and South Poles.

You may have heard someone say they were waiting for a fog to "burn off" before going out in a car. Although fog doesn't really burn away, it does eventually disappear thanks to the Sun's heat. As the Sun heats the ground, the fog begins to evaporate, starting with the outside edges of the foggy area.

Fog is probably the top weather phenomenon used in horror movies. Monsters lurk in the fog in dozens of movies, and you may even have seen a fog machine or two while trick-or-treating in your neighborhood. Why is fog so creepy? Dense fog makes it really difficult to see. So adding fog to a movie makes it easy for the film to hide scary villains . . . until they pop out suddenly.

In real life, fog probably isn't hiding a monster or a creepy dude with a chain saw. However, fog can still be dangerous for other reasons. For example, in dense fog you might not be able to see well enough to drive safely or to find your way on foot.

What determines visibility in the fog? It has a lot to do with the amount of water vapor in the air and the size of the water droplets that form the fog (bigger droplets mean lower visibility). Also, in an area with lots of smoke and pollution in the air, fog can become very dense even without much water vapor.

Take Control/Get Involved!

All right, let's grab our supplies and get ready to go into the fog! Here, we'll be making our own fog, making our own smog, and trying to figure out the best way to see through a foggy night.

1. Fog in a Jar

Quick Query

The Big Idea: Fog forms when water vapor in the air condenses into water drop-lets. In this experiment, you'll change the air pressure in a bottle to cause the same effect. What do you think will happen when the glove is thrust into the jar? What will happen when the glove is pulled out of the jar?

CAUTIONS: Ask an adult lab partner to help you with lighting the match, and be careful not to break the glass jar.

Materials:

- Water
- Wide-mouthed glass jar, big enough for you to fit your hand inside
- Rubber glove
- Matches

The Steps:

1. Practice your setup. Pour a very small amount of water into the jar. The bottom should be just barely covered with water. Put the fingers of the glove down inside the jar, turn the open wrist end inside out, and stretch the opening of the glove over the opening of the jar. This should seal the jar.

continued →

2. Take the glove off the jar. Now that you've practiced, you'll do the experiment.

3. Light a match and throw it into the jar. As quickly as you can, seal the jar with the glove the same way you did in step 1.

4. Quickly put your hand partially into the fingers of the glove and pull upward gently. Be careful not to pull the glove hard enough to break the seal on the jar. Observe what happens.

5. Push the glove back into the bottle where it started. Observe what happens.

Observations: What happened when you pulled the glove out of the jar? What happened when you pushed the glove back into the jar?

Kick It Up a Notch: Try doing this experiment again, but move the glove in and out of the jar more slowly. Can you find the exact point at which the fog begins to form?

The Hows and Whys: The water at the bottom of the jar begins to evaporate, forming water vapor. When you pull the glove out, the air in the jar expands and becomes cooler. As the water molecules cool down, they move more slowly, causing the water vapor to start to condense. The smoke particles from the burning match give the water vapor something to condense on, forming bigger droplets and denser fog. Fog often forms near mountaintops because the air pressure is lower at higher elevations.

2. Smog in a Jar

The Big Idea: The word "smog"—a heavy, dark fog containing smoke or chemical pollution—was created by combining the words "smoke" and "fog." Smog can occur for several reasons, including water droplets condensing on particles of soot in the air. In this experiment, you'll get to watch one kind of smog form in a jar. What do you think will happen when you put the ice cubes on top of the jar?

CAUTIONS: Ask an adult lab partner to help you with lighting the match.

Materials:

- Water
- Wide-mouthed glass jar with lid
- Matches
- Ice cubes

The Steps:

1. Pour a small amount of water into the jar. Put on the lid and shake the jar. Then remove the lid and pour out the water.

2. Light a match and throw it into the jar. Put the lid back on the jar.

3. Quickly put ice cubes on top of the jar lid. Add as many as will fit.

4. Sit back and observe what happens over the next few minutes.

continued →

Observations: What happened after you added the match to the jar? What changed after you added ice to the jar lid?

Kick It Up a Notch: Try the experiment without the match. Does the fog still form? If so, does it look any different?

The Hows and Whys: Fog and clouds form more quickly when water vapor can condense on particles in the air. When there is a lot of smoke and pollution in the air, it can cause the formation of the polluted fog we call smog. In our experiment, we used smoke from a match to add particles to the environment. In real life, car exhaust and smoke from factories add many particles to our atmosphere. This is one reason that some large cities with tons of traffic end up with smog problems.

3. Seeing Through the Fog

Take It Outside

The Big Idea: Fog lamps are special lights on some cars that can be found below the regular headlights. How do fog lamps on a car work? Go out on a foggy day and test it out! In this experiment, you'll shine a flashlight up high, at waist level, and near the ground. What happens when the light hits the fog? And which level of light do you think would make it easiest to see the markings on the road?

CAUTIONS: Have an adult lab partner go with you. Do not walk out onto a road, driveway, or parking lot when visibility is low. Be sure that you are standing somewhere you know is safe while you make your observations.

Materials:

- A foggy evening/morning
- Flashlight
- Pen or pencil

The Steps:

1. Go outside on a foggy evening or morning when it is dark. Choose a safe location where you will be able to see some kind of markings on the ground.

2. Shine the flashlight directly in front of you. With the flashlight in this position, can you see anything in front of you? Can you see any markings on the ground? Would you say that visibility is good, okay, bad, or very bad?

continued →

3. Now crouch down near the ground and shine the flashlight straight in front of you. Answer the same questions you answered in step 2.

4. Next, stand all the way up and hold the flashlight above your head.

Shine the light forward, but keep the light at the same level above your head. Again, answer the questions from step 2.

5. Go inside and record your results in the data table below.

Observations: Which flashlight position made it easiest to see markings on the ground? Which position made it easiest to see directly in front of you?

Kick It Up a Notch: Try this experiment again with several different types of lights. Try flashlights with incandescent bulbs and LED bulbs. Which provides the best visibility?

The Hows and Whys: Fog lamps on cars are designed to work differently from headlights. Fog lamps shine down onto the road so that drivers can see the road beneath the fog and stay safely in their own lanes. Cars are built with fog lamps because regular headlights often shine up and into the fog, which is bad for visibility. The light from the headlights reflects off the fog, making it difficult to see. You probably experienced this reflection when you shined the light right in front of you in this experiment.

LEVEL OF FLASHLIGHT	LEVEL OF VISIBILITY
Low	
Middle	
High	

CHAPTER 8

Dust Storms

When an area has dry soil and strong winds, it may experience dust storms. A **dust storm** happens when the winds are so strong that they pick up particles of soil, suspend them in the air for a while, and eventually drop the soil particles somewhere else.

Dust storms are most common in very dry places, such as the desert regions of northern Africa and the Arabian Peninsula. In the United States, they're most common in southwestern states such as Arizona and New Mexico.

Have you ever experienced a dust storm in your home climate?

HOW DOES IT DO THAT?

A dust storm usually starts with—you guessed it—a storm. Thunderstorms can create very strong winds that pick up dust, sand, and soil from the dry ground. These dust storms can travel fast: 20 to 60 miles per hour. Once the particles are lifted off the ground, they rise higher and higher in the atmosphere in upward-moving air currents, called **updrafts**.

Then strong winds high in the atmosphere really take the dust particles for a ride. Depending on the size of the particles, they can stay suspended in the atmosphere for anywhere from a few hours to 10 days or more. During this time, the dust can travel hundreds or thousands of miles away from where it was picked up. Eventually, the dust particles settle out of the atmosphere and fall to the ground.

It might seem like a few dust particles blowing around here and there aren't a very big deal. Yet this traveling dust can have a big impact on our planet's ecosystems. For example, scientists estimate that each year 20 million tons of dust are blown from the Sahara Desert in Africa all the way to the Amazon River basin in South America. This dust brings essential nutrients to the plants and animals of the Amazon rainforests.

Although dust storms have an important role in Earth's ecosystems, the blowing dust can also be a major nuisance, and even a hazard. First of all, dust in the air is bad for human health. Very small dust particles—the ones small enough to be breathed in—can get stuck in your nose, mouth, and sinuses. These small particles can cause breathing and heart problems, including disorders such as pneumonia, asthma, and cardiovascular disease.

Dust storms can also have impacts on Earth's weather patterns. You might remember from chapter 4 that clouds form more quickly and easily when particles called aerosols are in the atmosphere.

These particles serve as a "seed" for water-droplet formation; water vapor encounters the particles and immediately begins to form droplets around them. Particles from dust storms are examples of aerosols. So dust storms can have a major effect on local cloud formation. The different sizes of dust particles can change how the clouds reflect the Sun's heat, affecting local temperatures.

Human activities are having an impact on Earth's dust storms. Forests and grasses have roots that keep soil in the ground. When people clear forests and grasslands for farms, houses, and other buildings, more of the soil is exposed, meaning it can be easily picked up into a dust storm. In addition, the warming climate makes soil dry out and plants die, exposing even more soil to the wind.

Strike a Pose

Dust storms can have a remarkable impact on landscapes. The photos below—from real dust storms—are both cool and devastating. Let's take a look at what dust storms look like from space, from the sky, and from the ground:

Dust storms carry so much dust and soil that they can even be seen from space! This image, taken by a satellite orbiting Earth, shows winds carrying dust from the Sahara Desert 1,000 miles or more into the Atlantic Ocean.

This photo, taken from a helicopter, shows a dust storm

approaching and hitting Phoenix, Arizona. It moves in like a wall of dust, just ahead of a thunderstorm. The photographer and pilot were able to get to safety after taking this photo, but flying airplanes and helicopters in dust storms can be very dangerous.

This well-known photograph showing a building buried in sand after a dust storm was taken in Oklahoma in 1936. At this time, America's southern prairie states were experiencing a drought. They were also hit with many dust storms that were so severe, they were often called "black blizzards." Because of the choking storms, people started referring to the region as the Dust Bowl. The impact of the Dust Bowl time period damaged the area's ecosystem and farms for many years.

To the Extremes!

It may not be too surprising that the Sahara Desert is dusty. In fact, more than half of the dust that ends up in the ocean was lifted from the Sahara. A specific region of the southern Sahara called the Bodélé Depression is the dustiest place on Earth. It has dust storms carrying plumes of dust into the air more than 100 days per year.

Can people live in the dusty Sahara? Absolutely! Approximately 2.5 million people live in the Sahara Desert. They either live permanently near sources of water, or they travel around from place to place to graze their herds of sheep, goats, or camels.

Although dust storms can happen in most climates, they are unlikely to occur in an area with lots of moisture and plants, like a forest or a rainforest.

Take Control/Get Involved!

Dust storms can be dangerous to experience in real life, but we can learn about them by doing experiments at home. Here, we'll study how wind speed affects the pattern of dust spread by a dust storm, see how different types of soil behave in a dust storm, and then try to predict which regions are at greatest risk of dust storms. Let's get dusty!

1. Tabletop Dust Storm

Quick Query

The Big Idea: Air seems like it's almost nothing at all, but it is strong enough to carry particles—and enough particles in the air create a dust storm. In this experiment, you'll make your own dust storm by blowing into a box full of flour. How does the path of the flour change if you blow softly or with more force? In what directions does the flour move?

CAUTIONS: Be careful not to breathe in any of the flour dust!

Materials:

- Flour
- Clear plastic box with a hole in one end
- Notebook or paper
- Pen or pencil

The Steps:

1. Add a small amount of flour to the bottom of the clear box.

2. Blow into the hole in the box. Try making a gentle breeze first. Observe where the flour goes and how long the particles of flour stay suspended in the air. Record your observations.

3. Next, blow a big gust of wind into the box. Observe where the flour goes and how long the particles of flour stay in the air this time. Record your observations.

continued →

Observations: Did the particles of flour stay in the air longer with the big gust or with the gentle breeze? How were the scattering patterns of the dust different in the two types of wind?

Kick It Up a Notch: Try the experiment again, but angle your breath upward and downward to simulate updrafts and downdrafts. Will those change how long the particles are suspended in the air?

The Hows and Whys: You probably noticed that the harder you blew on the flour, the more flour went into the air and the longer it stayed suspended there. This is also true of dust storms, where big gusts of wind pull tons of dust and sand into the sky.

2. Dust Storm vs. Sandstorm

The Big Idea: The soil on Earth's surface is different all over the world. How does each kind of soil behave in the wind? In this experiment, you'll see how dust (represented by powdered sugar), sand, and soil blow differently in the wind. Which do you think will blow farthest in the wind created by the hair dryer?

  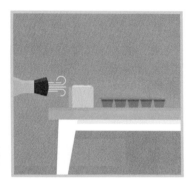

CAUTIONS: Ask a grown-up lab partner for help with plugging in and using the hair dryer.

Materials:

- Blocks of wood
- Ice-cube tray
- Sand
- Hair dryer
- Soil from the ground near your home
- Powdered sugar
- Pen or pencil

The Steps:

1. Find a flat location near an electrical outlet. Make a small platform with the wooden blocks. Place the ice-cube tray a few inches in front of the platform. The platform should sit slightly higher than the top of the ice-cube tray.

2. Place a small pile of sand on the platform and plug in the hair dryer nearby.

3. Point the hair dryer at the pile of sand and toward the ice-cube tray. Turn on the hair dryer for about 5 to 10 seconds. Observe where in the ice-cube tray the sand lands.

continued →

4. Next, place a small pile of soil from the ground near your home on the platform. Perform the same procedure as in step 3. Observe where the soil ends up.

5. Then, place a small pile of powdered sugar on the platform. Perform the same procedure as in step 3. Observe where the sugar ends up.

6. Look at the ice-cube tray and observe how each material traveled in the wind created by the hair dryer. Record your results in the data table below.

Observations: Which material traveled farthest in the wind? Which material spread into more of the ice-cube compartments?

Kick It Up a Notch: Try the same experiment with a variety of materials other than sand and soil. Try small pebbles, garden mulch, or any other material you're curious about.

The Hows and Whys: In a dust storm, the smallest, lightest particles are usually carried farthest by the wind—sometimes thousands of miles. If you look at the soil and the sand you used, you'll probably notice that whichever of the two had smaller particles ended up in the farthest ice-cube compartment.

MATERIAL	NUMBER OF ICE CUBE COMPARTMENTS WITH "DUST" IN THEM AFTER USING THE HAIR DRYER
Sand	
Soil	
Powdered sugar	

3. Mapping Dust Storms

Take It Outside

The Big Idea: Dust storms are caused by a few specific geographic traits. Regions with very dry soil are the most likely to experience dust storms. In this experiment, you'll take a look at satellite images of Earth and try to find the regions that are most likely to have dust storms. What do you think those regions will look like in a satellite view? Then you'll do an Internet search of regions prone to dust storms to check your predictions.

CAUTIONS: Have a grown-up lab partner help you with Internet searches on the computer, tablet, or smartphone.

Materials:

- Computer, tablet, or smartphone with access to satellite images of Earth and information on the geographic traits of different regions

The Steps:

1. Look at a satellite image of Earth. Closely examine the color and makeup of each region you see. For example, does this region look mountainous? Is it mostly green, meaning it has lots of trees and vegetation?

2. Based on the appearance of the regions in the satellite image (and any additional research you've done), predict which regions might be prone to dust storms. Record your predictions in the data table on the next page.

3. Do an Internet search to see if dust storms are common in the regions you predicted.

continued →

Observations: What criteria did you use to decide whether or not a region would have dust storms? Were your predictions accurate?

Kick It Up a Notch: Does the region where you live experience a lot of dust storms? Look at the area around you and make a list of the things you think make your region prone to dust storms or dust-storm proof.

The Hows and Whys: Generally, regions that have lots of dust storms are desert areas. In a satellite image, they would be wide-open spaces that appear to be a sort of tan or brown color from above. Areas that appear green and lush in a satellite image are usually full of plants and trees. Plants and trees have roots that dig into the soil, making it more difficult for the wind to pick up particles and carry them into the air.

PREDICTION: REGIONS PRONE TO DUST STORMS	CRITERIA USED	RESEARCH: IS REGION ACTUALLY PRONE TO DUST STORMS?
Region 1		
Region 2		
Region 3		
Region 4		
Region 5		
Region 6		

PART THREE

NATURAL DISASTERS: WE'RE NOT IN KANSAS ANYMORE

We've all had times when bad weather changed our plans for the day. But weather can be much, much worse. When weather events destroy homes, roads, and cities, it completely changes the lives of the people who live nearby. A devastating weather phenomenon like this is considered a **natural disaster**.

Hurricanes, floods, wildfires, and droughts are all types of weather-related natural disasters. These events can cause shortages of things that people need, such as housing, food, and medical care. Every year close to 160 million people on Earth are affected by natural disasters.

Unfortunately, we can't prevent weather-related natural disasters from happening. But meteorologists have studied these weather events and can help give us a heads-up when they are likely to happen.

For example, have you ever heard of "hurricane season" or "tornado season"? Conditions for these storms can occur almost any time of year, but there are time periods—seasons—when they are more likely to happen. Meteorologists have found that most hurricanes on the Atlantic coast of the United States occur between June and November. Similarly, they can predict that most tornadoes in the Southern Plains states will form in May and June.

Meteorologists also use a variety of tools to measure conditions in the atmosphere that can indicate that a very extreme weather event is on its way. They also try to predict which areas might be hit hardest by the disastrous phenomenon. Forecasts and weather alerts can then help people prepare to evacuate or get to shelter to stay safe.

Ask your parents or teachers if they have ever had to prepare for a big storm, such as Hurricane Irma, Hurricane Sandy, or the very active tornado season of 2011. How did they feel during that time? What did they do to feel prepared?

CHAPTER 9

Tornadoes

A **tornado** is a spinning tube of air that extends from a thunderstorm cloud in the sky all the way down to the ground. The rotating winds of a tornado move very fast—sometimes more than 300 miles per hour. Tornado winds are very dangerous because they can pick up and throw debris. Just as you may have seen in the movie *The Wizard of Oz*, these winds are strong enough to pick up and destroy cars, trees, homes, and other buildings. Very powerful tornadoes have even destroyed entire towns.

Most tornadoes in the United States form in the Great Plains—a region that includes parts of North Dakota, South Dakota, Wyoming, Nebraska, Kansas, Colorado, Oklahoma, Texas, and New Mexico. Because this area experiences tornadoes so frequently, it is often called Tornado Alley.

Why are tornadoes so common in the Great Plains? Here, cold, dry air from the north meets warm, moist air from the south. When the two air masses meet, clouds—and eventually thunderstorms—can form. Tornadoes result from specific kinds of thunderstorms. Most thunderstorms form in the spring and summer months, so that's when tornadoes usually happen, too. This is sometimes called tornado season.

If conditions are right, tornadoes can form almost anywhere in the United States. However, there aren't many tornadoes in the Pacific Northwest or the Northeast. Have you ever heard of a tornado happening near where you live?

HOW DOES IT DO THAT?

We know that clouds form when warm, moist air rises in the atmosphere, cools, and condenses into water droplets. We also know that tornadoes stem from thunderstorm clouds. But how exactly does a tornado form?

Meteorologists aren't totally sure. Almost all tornadoes come from thunderstorms, but only a small fraction of thunderstorms actually cause tornadoes. And we don't yet know exactly what makes a tornado-forming thunderstorm different from a regular thunderstorm.

Here is what we do know: Tornadoes often form from spinning thunderstorms called **supercells**.

A supercell thunderstorm looks like a giant anvil in the sky. They are not very common. But when they do form, they can cause very severe weather such as strong winds and hail—and occasionally tornadoes.

All thunderstorms form when warm air rises, creating an upward wind called an updraft, and cold air sinks, creating a downward wind called a **downdraft**. This is how supercells form, too.

However, supercells are different from the average thunderstorm. In a supercell, winds on the ground and winds much higher up—about 20,000 feet above the ground—blow in different directions. This creates a rolling, horizontal tube of air. Next, the storm's updraft pulls the rolling tube of air upright. This movement creates a spinning thunderstorm—a supercell.

Only about 30 percent of supercells actually form tornadoes. Scientists don't yet understand what makes these special tornado-producing storms different from other supercells. But they are always designing experiments to learn more!

Tornadoes produce some of the fastest winds on Earth. Some are only a few feet wide, but others are wider than a football field. Tornadoes can last anywhere from several seconds to several hours.

Meteorologists often don't know how fast or wide a tornado really was until they study the path of the damage after the storm. Once the storm is over, they look at what is destroyed and what is still standing. Were trees knocked over, while houses are still standing? Were small houses destroyed, but large buildings like hospitals untouched?

After collecting this information, meteorologists can estimate the wind speeds of the storm and rate the tornado. Tornados are rated using the Enhanced Fujita scale, which goes from 0 to 5. An EF-0 tornado has estimated wind speeds of about 65 to 85 miles per hour, while an EF-5 has wind speeds of 200 miles per hour or more.

Meteorologists are constantly keeping an eye on the weather to see if conditions are right for a tornado. If a thunderstorm is spotted when conditions seem right, you'll probably see a "tornado watch" issued. But if a tornado is actually spotted in your area, you'll hear a "tornado warning." In either case, pay attention to warnings, updates, and guidance from your local weather experts.

Pop Culture Quiz!

One of the most popular weather movies of all time was the 1996 film *Twister*. As with most movies, while some events were based in fact, there were also many "do not try this at home" moments. Take this little true/false quiz to learn more about what is real and what is Hollywood storytelling.

People drive around in cars and trucks chasing tornadoes.

True! Many meteorologists and videographers flock to the Great Plains states in the spring and summer to chase storms. Some storm chasers come to do research and collect ground data, like the scientists in the film. Other storm chasers are mostly there to catch the wild storms on video. They then sell the videos and photos to television stations or post them on the Internet.

You can hide from a tornado inside a car.

False! A character in the movie tries to seek shelter from a tornado inside a car. In real life, this would be a terrible idea. Tornado winds are so strong that they can pick up and throw a car, destroying the vehicle and seriously injuring any people inside. The best place to take shelter during a tornado is in the basement of a house or building. If you don't have a basement, take shelter in a room near the center of the house that doesn't have windows.

On March 3, 2019, a strong storm system caused approximately 40 tornadoes to tear through the southeastern United States. The tornadoes caused a great deal of damage in parts of Alabama, Florida, and Georgia.

One tornado that day was rated EF-4—meaning that there were winds of 166 miles per hour or more. This was the most dangerous tornado in the system. It left a miles-long trail of destroyed trees, homes, and other buildings. Because of just this one tornado, 23 people died and many others were injured.

After these storms, towns were completely destroyed. Although a disaster like a tornado is devastating, people in affected communities came together to clean up debris and help out their neighbors in need.

Disaster-relief workers and community volunteers loaded debris into garbage trucks to be hauled away. But cleanup is only one part of the process. Rebuilding takes a much longer time. Even a year after the storm, many people in affected communities still weren't able to move back to the exact places they used to call home.

Take Control/Get Involved!

In the experiments that follow, you'll learn how meteorologists determine the location of big storms, make a storm in a container, and design a tornado-safe house. Let's get ready to (safely) learn about tornadoes!

1. Doppler Effect

Quick Query

The Big Idea: Meteorologists use Doppler radar to figure out the speed and direction of moving objects, such as thunderstorms. Doppler radar improves weather forecasts because it can determine the speed and direction of winds. That can help predict how strong a storm will be and where it will travel next. In this experiment, you'll experience the Doppler effect using a razor and an audio-recording device. How do you think the sound of the razor will change as it gets closer or farther from the microphone?

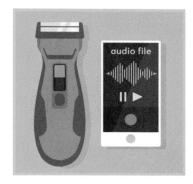  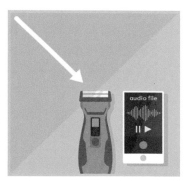

CAUTIONS: You may want to have a grown-up lab partner help you operate the electric razor.

Materials:

- Battery-operated electric razor
- Audio-recording device or app on a smartphone, tablet, or computer

The Steps:

1. Turn on the razor. Hold the razor next to the microphone of your device, and record the sound. Do not move the razor as you record.

2. Play the recording you just made to make sure it sounds the same as the original razor sound.

continued →

3. Turn on the razor a second time and press record on the audio-recording device or app. This time, move the razor closer to and farther away from the microphone a few times.

4. Play the two recordings and observe how they are different.

Observations: How did the razor sound when it was held still next to the microphone? How did its sound differ when you moved it toward and away from the microphone?

Kick It Up a Notch: Try the experiment again, but this time move the razor back-and-forth past the microphone quickly, then again slowly. Play the sound back for someone else. Can they tell how the movements were different based only on the sounds?

The Hows and Whys: The razor sounds higher-pitched as it moves toward the microphone and lower-pitched as it moves away. This is because of a phenomenon called the Doppler effect. Sound is made up of waves. As an object making sound moves toward you, the waves are squeezed closer together. This makes the sound higher pitched. As the object moves away from you, the waves stretch out, resulting in a lower-pitched sound.

Meteorologists use this effect in a tool called Doppler radar. Doppler radar uses radio waves, which bounce off thunderstorm clouds and back to the receiver. Like sound waves, radio waves experience the Doppler effect. Meteorologists can study how the reflected signal changed from the original signal. This helps them figure out how far away a storm is, how fast it's moving, and whether it is a rotating supercell.

2. How Does a Storm Form?

The Big Idea: In general, storms form where masses of warm air meet masses of cool air in the atmosphere. In this experiment, you'll recreate this phenomenon using color-coded warm and cool water. What do you think will happen to the warm and cool water when they are combined in the clear plastic box?

CAUTIONS: Be careful with the food coloring, as it can stain clothing and carpets.

Materials:

- Water
- Cups
- Blue and red food coloring
- Spoon
- Ice-cube tray
- Clear plastic shoe box

The Steps:

1. Pour some water into a cup and add a few drops of blue food coloring. Use the spoon to stir the mixture. Pour your blue water into the ice-cube tray, then place it in the freezer until it's frozen solid.

2. After the blue ice cubes have frozen, pour water that is barely warm into the clear plastic shoe box. Add a few drops of red food coloring to one side of the warm water in the box.

3. Add 3 or 4 blue ice cubes to the side of the box opposite to the red-colored water.

4. Observe what happens.

continued →

Observations: What happened as the blue ice cubes began to melt?

Kick It Up a Notch: Try a few different combinations of temperatures. For example, what happens if you use cold water in the shoe box instead of lukewarm water? What happens if you use hot water?

The Hows and Whys: In nature, thunderstorms can form when cold air masses meet warm air masses. The cold air masses sink down, pushing the warm air masses up. You can see the same thing happening in the experiment when the cold blue water pushes underneath the lukewarm red water. Where the red and blue water meet is where unstable air would appear in the atmosphere. This is the spot where thunderstorms form.

3. Keep the Outside from Getting In

Take It Outside

The Big Idea: Tornadoes have very high wind speeds, which can cause damage to houses and buildings. Engineers and architects can take steps to design tornado-safe rooms and buildings. Grab a pencil and paper (or a computer drawing program) and design a tornado-safe room of your own. Here are a few tornado-safe features:

- The room should have no windows.

- The room should not be prone to flooding.

- The walls and ceiling should be safe from wind and debris flying at up to 250 miles per hour.

- The door should open into the room so that you can still open it even if the floor outside is blocked by debris.

- The room should have a strong foundation.

CAUTIONS: None! This activity is safe for all ages.

Materials:

- Pencil
- Paper

continued →

The Steps:

1. Read the list of features needed for a tornado-safe building on the previous page.

2. Use pencil and paper to design a house or building of any kind that would be safe to shelter in during a tornado.

Observations: What features were needed to make the building safe during a tornado? Was it difficult to add these features while also making sure there were bathrooms, bedrooms, and all the other normal parts of a house?

Kick It Up a Notch: Try actually building your design with plastic building blocks. Is your design safe—and still livable?

The Hows and Whys: Tornadoes bring with them strong winds, intense rains, and sometimes even hail. The best place to be safe from tornadoes is in a basement— and one that isn't at risk of flooding. The next best option is a room near the center of a house without any windows. Why? Tornadoes fling debris that can shatter windows, making flying bits of broken glass that can injure the people inside. Think about your own house and where you might go during a tornado or other extreme storm.

CHAPTER 10

Hurricanes

Hurricanes are some of the strongest and most recognizable storms on Earth. From above, a hurricane looks like a spinning pinwheel with a hole in the middle. However, from the ground they're quite scary. With wind speeds of up to 200 miles per hour, these violent storms can destroy houses and rip trees right out of the ground. They are also huge, often measuring about 300 miles across.

These giant storms begin as thunderstorms just north or south of the equator. Why there? The warm, tropical water creates moisture and heat that fuel the storm. Hurricanes usually form in tropical climates, such as off the western coast of Africa or in the Caribbean Sea. A hurricane can form at any time of year if the conditions are right, but most hurricanes in the Atlantic happen from June to November. So that time of year is called hurricane season.

Where do hurricanes never form? Hurricanes can't form right at the equator. They also rarely form off the coast of Europe or off the West Coast of the United States.

Do you live in a climate that has hurricanes?

HOW DOES IT DO THAT?

Hurricanes (and tropical cyclones and typhoons) begin over warm ocean waters. The tropical waters just north and south of the equator create warm, moist air that rises into the atmosphere. As we learned in previous chapters, water vapor cools as it rises, becoming water droplets that form clouds.

With the warm, moist air continuing to rise off the ocean, clouds grow bigger and bigger, forming thunderstorm clouds. Many thunderstorm clouds form just north and south of the equator.

But how do thunderstorm clouds turn into a spinning hurricane?

The rotation of the storms is an effect of Earth's rotation. Because Earth always spins in the same direction, winds—and other things traveling in straight lines—begin to veer in one direction. Winds in the Northern Hemisphere tend to turn toward the right, and those in the Southern Hemisphere turn toward the left.

As we learned earlier, in chapter 3, this is called the Coriolis effect, and it's what turns a cluster of thunderstorm clouds into a spinning hurricane. Because of the Coriolis effect, hurricanes in the Northern Hemisphere rotate counterclockwise. Hurricanes in the Southern Hemisphere, on the other hand, rotate clockwise.

Once the wind speeds in this rotating storm reach 39 miles per hour, meteorologists call it a tropical storm. And once the storm reaches 74 miles per hour, it is called a hurricane.

Cyclone, Typhoon, or Hurricane?

You've probably heard of big hurricanes hitting islands in the Caribbean or the coast of Florida, but did you know these big storms happen in tropical areas all over the world? It's true! However, they have different names depending on where they happen.

For example, if the storm happens in the North Atlantic Ocean or eastern Pacific Ocean, it's a hurricane. But if the same type of storm happens in the South Atlantic Ocean or Indian Ocean, it's called a **tropical cyclone**. Ever heard of a **typhoon**? That is a hurricane-like storm occurring in the western Pacific Ocean.

In the center of a hurricane is an area of relative calm called the eye. The eye is an area of low air pressure with calm winds and no rain. However, just outside the eye is the eye wall. The eye wall is far from calm—it has some of the storm's strongest winds. Spiraling out from the eye wall are bands of thunderstorms called rain bands.

A hurricane picks up its energy from the warm, moist air over the tropical ocean water. As long as the storm stays over warm water, its winds will continue to get stronger. Storms begin to lose their strength once they encounter colder waters. A hurricane also starts to weaken when it encounters land.

However, when a hurricane reaches land, it is still very powerful. Wind and rain from hurricanes are very destructive and can damage or destroy houses and other buildings in their paths.

Weather IRL

The 2017 Atlantic hurricane season set lots of records—and not in a good way. The ocean waters were especially warm that year, fueling many hurricanes. In fact, it was the most active hurricane season in US history, and the most expensive.

Four major hurricanes caused a lot of the damage that year. The hurricanes were named Harvey, Irma, Maria, and Nate. Hurricane Harvey hit the coast of Texas in August of 2017 with 100 mph winds and up to five feet of rain, which caused major flooding.

A few weeks later, Hurricane Irma hit land in Florida and the Virgin Islands, causing lots of damage and leaving approximately 16 million people without electricity. Later, Hurricane Maria devastated Puerto Rico. Three months after the hurricane hit, more than half of the island still didn't have electrical power.

Then, in October, Hurricane Nate arrived on land in Central America and the United States, causing hundreds of millions of dollars in damage.

How long did it take to recover from these storms? It can take years to rebuild communities after major storms like these. Electricity and roads can sometimes be restored within weeks or months. However, it has taken people in affected regions—such as Texas and Puerto Rico—several years to clean up the debris and begin repairing and rebuilding houses.

Another scary result of hurricanes can be storm surge. Storm surge occurs when the level of the ocean rises abnormally high because of the storm's winds and movement. Some hurricanes produce storm surges higher than 25 feet. Sometimes the flooding from storm surge ends up causing more damage than the hurricane itself.

Scientists have observed how hurricanes are changing as our planet undergoes climate change. They predict that as Earth warms, hurricanes will become more intense—and the number of intense hurricanes will increase. Rising sea levels are another result of climate change. So scientists predict that these higher seas will also cause more intense flooding during hurricanes.

Take Control/Get Involved!

Hurricanes are dangerous storms, but we can learn more about them by safely doing experiments at home. In this chapter, we'll create a tool to monitor wind speeds, study the effects of storm surge, and track real storms over the ocean. Take a look at the materials lists to make sure you have everything you need, and let's get started!

1. Wind Spinner

Quick Query

The Big Idea: Meteorologists use tools called anemometers to measure wind speed and direction from the ground. These tools help in studying many different types of weather. However, they can be especially helpful in determining how strong a hurricane is and where it's traveling. In this experiment, you'll use the spinning action of a fidget spinner toy and some sails made from paper and tape. What location near your house do you think will have the strongest wind?

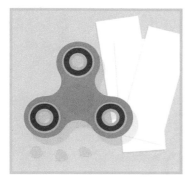  

CAUTIONS: Be careful when using scissors.

Materials:

- Ruler
- Paper
- Scissors
- Tape or poster putty
- Fidget spinner

The Steps:

1. Using the ruler, measure out three sails on your paper. Each sail should be a rectangle 5 cm (2 inches) by 10 cm (4 inches). Using your scissors, cut out each sail.

2. Place the paper rectangles so that the short sides are at the bottom and top. Label the corners of each rectangle with the numbers 1 through 4; start with the number 1

continued →

in the bottom left corner and go counterclockwise.

3. Place the corner labeled 1 in the center of the fidget spinner while pushing the area between 1 and 2 into the putty. Do this for all three rectangles.

4. Lift up each of the corners labeled 4. Stack the number 4's on top of one another with the corners of the paper pointing to the middle of the fidget spinner. Use tape to join the corners together in this way. Corners labeled 3 should be free and pointing to the outside of the fidget spinner.

5. Blow air into the sails or set the device outside in the wind to test it.

Observations: What did you notice when you placed your anemometer in the wind?

Kick It Up a Notch: Once you've made your anemometer, test wind speeds in several spots near your home. Do any areas act as wind tunnels, funneling the wind into one spot? Are there any areas where the wind is completely blocked?

The Hows and Whys: This type of anemometer works by catching the wind in the sails, which turns the fidget spinner. You can use this simple design to make a relative measurement of the wind. If the fidget spinner is moving fast, the winds are at higher speeds than when it is spinning slowly. However, if you wanted to know the exact wind speed, you'd need to do some special calculations based on the size of the fidget spinner.

2. The Big Wave

The Big Idea: A storm surge is a giant mass of water that comes ashore during a hurricane. This flood of water can cause a great deal of the damage from the storm. In this experiment, you'll create your own storm surge in a plastic tub indoors. When you create the wind, which area of the tub do you think will receive the most damage?

CAUTIONS: If using a hair dryer or a fan, remember to keep it away from the water. Do *not* get it wet.

Materials:

- 1 bag (40 to 50 pounds) play sand
- Large, low-sided plastic container, like an under-the-bed storage bin
- Water
- Sponges
- Items to represent houses
- Tiny toy animals, people, and cars
- Plastic straws
- Erasable markers
- Block of wood, fan, or hair dryer (something to make waves with)
- Paper towels

The Steps:

1. Place sand in one half of the long plastic container. The sand will represent land.

2. Slightly moisten the sand with water. Use a finger to create a curvy river down the center of the sand. As the river gets closer to the part that will be the ocean, you can create several smaller curvy rivers branching off.

continued →

3. On the sides of the river, create low areas in the sand. Place pieces of damp sponge in these areas, which will represent salt marshes. You can also create marshes—grassy wetlands—away from the ocean area.

4. Using moistened sand, create an oval-shaped island several inches away from the mouth of your river in the ocean area. The island should not block the mouth of the river.

5. Add water slowly to the ocean side of the container. Add enough water that the island is surrounded and the mouth of river contains some water.

6. Add houses, animals, people, and cars to the island and along the river. You can use plastic straws to place houses on stilts.

7. On the outside of the container, use an erasable marker to place a mark every half inch from the edge of the ocean to the end of the land. Number each mark starting with 0, then 1, 2, 3, etc.

8. If using a block of wood, gently tap the water in the ocean by moving the block up and down to create mild waves. If using a hair dryer or a fan, turn it on low. Hold the hair dryer or fan some distance away from the water to make gentle waves. Use the paper towels if any water spills.

9. Observe what happens.

Observations: What happens to your island, the marshes, and the land behind the island? What happens to the people, cars, animals, and houses?

Kick it up a Notch: Try creating bigger waves by moving the block up and down faster or turning the hair dryer or fan to a higher setting. Try creating more islands or more marshes. What happens if the island is farther away from the mainland?

The Hows and Whys: Building barrier islands—like the oval island you created in this exercise—is a way that we can prevent storm surge from destroying a coastal community. Barrier islands absorb energy from waves so that the waves are weaker once they reach the coast. Grassy marshes—represented by the sponges in this experiment—can also absorb energy and reduce the height of waves.

3. Track a Hurricane

Take It Outside

The Big Idea: Hurricane season in North America happens every summer as tropical storms pick up speed from warm oceans, with some eventually turning into hurricanes. In this experiment, you'll follow news reports of tropical storms and try to predict which ones will become hurricanes. Which factors do you think will fuel and strengthen a tropical storm?

CAUTIONS: Always check with an adult lab partner before using the Internet.

Materials:

- TV or computer with Internet access to track tropical storms
- Pen or pencil

The Steps:

1. Watch the news on TV or use the Internet to find out what tropical storms are forming in the Atlantic Ocean.

2. Track each tropical storm every day and record its location, wind speed, ocean temperature, etc. in the data table on the next page.

3. Make a prediction whether each tropical storm will become a hurricane or not. Write down your predictions.

4. Record whether each tropical storm turned into a hurricane or not in the data table.

Observations: What factors were important for a tropical storm to become a hurricane? Wind speed? Ocean temperature?

continued →

Kick It Up a Notch: Look back at records of tropical storms that turned into hurricanes in previous years. Use this information to help you make your predictions.

The Hows and Whys: Meteorologists use satellite images to track where tropical storms are, but they also use wind speed and direction measurements in the middle of the atmosphere to determine which way the storm will move and how fast it's moving. This generally allows them to get a good idea of where the storm will go. However, storms can also be unpredictable. For example, meteorologists try to give a hurricane warning a day or two before a storm hits land. But sometimes a storm gets stuck in an area with no wind and stays in the same spot for days before moving on to the coast. So don't feel bad if it takes some time to perfect your predictions.

TROPICAL STORM NAME	LOCATION	WIND SPEED	OCEAN TEMPERATURE	PREDICTION: HURRICANE OR NO?	RESULT: HURRICANE OR NO?

CHAPTER 11

Wildfires

Fires are an important and natural part of many ecosystems. For example, when thick, dry brush burns away in a fire, it makes room for young, healthy plants to thrive. And certain species of trees, like jack pines, need the high heat of a fire to release their seeds.

Wildfires are fires that are fueled by plants and trees. They can get out of control, spreading very fast and destroying nearby homes and environments. In nature, wildfires are generally started by lightning. However, many wildfires aren't natural at all—they are often sparked by human activity.

As our climate changes, warmer temperatures and drier plants can easily allow a small fire to burn out of control. When wildfires get out of control, they can spread incredibly quickly, becoming very dangerous for communities of people and wildlife.

Wildfires often start in rural areas, far away from cities, where there is plenty of grass and brush to burn. They are also more likely to start in areas with high winds, high temperatures, and not much precipitation. These conditions dry out trees and plants, making them burn more easily.

One place that never sees wildfires is Antarctica. Since the continent is mostly made up of ice and rock, there is little to burn there.

HOW DOES IT DO THAT?

Wildfires all begin the same way: with a spark. In nature, this spark can happen when a lightning bolt hits a field of dry grass. However, human activities are to blame for many sparks. Fireworks and campfires are two of the most common causes of wildfires.

A wildfire starts when the spark encounters fuel—usually plants, such as grasses, brush, and twigs. Wildfires can happen almost anywhere with enough fuel, including grasslands, savannahs, and forests. Places with overgrown forests, lots of dead leaves, or thick vegetation can give a fire a big boost of fuel, causing it to quickly grow out of control.

However, it's not just vegetation above the ground that can fuel a fire. Roots and other plant material below ground can also feed fires. A **ground fire** is a type of fire that burns below ground, releasing smoke into the air.

Ground fires can burn and smolder for months before anyone even sees a flame above ground. When the flames start burning leaves and grasses above ground, it becomes a **surface fire**. Fires can even break out in the leaves at the tops of trees and shrubs in a forest. This kind of treetop blaze is called a **crown fire**.

What does all this have to do with weather? A lot, actually! Weather conditions have a big impact on how much and how quickly a wildfire grows. Warm temperatures, fast winds, and below-average rainfall can all create dry and fire-prone conditions.

In hot weather, plant material like fallen sticks and leaves can be quickly dried out by heat from the Sun. This creates lots of fuel to help a fire start and spread. Warm outdoor temperatures also cause fuel to catch fire and burn faster. This is why most wildfires are strongest in the heat of the afternoon sun.

Unfortunately, as human activities contribute to climate change, wildfires are becoming more common. Warmer weather dries out vegetation, making it easier for it to catch fire. One result is that the fire season in California is now 75 days longer than it was just a few decades ago.

Wind is also a big factor in the formation and spread of wildfires. Fires need more than just a spark and fuel: They also need oxygen. When wind blows on a fire, it provides a big boost of oxygen, causing the fire to burn faster. Blowing wind can also change directions, unpredictably moving a fire from place to place.

Although we can't do anything to change the weather, there are steps that we can take to prevent wildfires from affecting our communities. Because fires require a spark and fuel to start, we can do our best to keep those two things under control.

Is It Weather or Climate?

As we learned earlier in this book, weather and climate are two different things—and the biggest difference is time. Weather describes the day-to-day outdoor conditions in an area, whereas climate is the average of weather conditions in a region over many, many years.

How do scientists combine years of weather information to determine a region's climate? It starts with millions of weather observations. All over the world, people—and remote weather stations—collect information about each day's weather. These observers collect and record information about the low and high temperatures for the day and measure any precipitation that falls.

Now, it takes some math to figure out how these observations relate to climate. Meteorologists and government agencies gather all of these local weather records and begin their calculations. For example, the daily average temperature in an area is calculated by finding the average of the low and high temperatures for each day, then finding the average of those average temperatures. They also add up all of the precipitation that fell each month.

Meteorologists can then compare these averages and totals with those from previous years in the same region to look for patterns. (For example, the data could show that in a particular region, January is usually rainy and cold, while August is hot and dry.) They also compare the conditions in a region to those in other regions nearby.

Why is this climate information important? There are many reasons. For example, decision-makers in cities and towns need this information to plan for energy and water usage, road maintenance, and safety in extreme weather events.

To prevent sparks, we can follow safety procedures and local rules when lighting campfires or using fireworks. And to keep the amount of fuel in check, there are a few things we can do. For example, we should always keep excess vegetation—fire fuel—away from houses and buildings. See a stack of leaves outside your garage? Clean it up right away! See some long, dry grass right next to your front door? Get out the lawnmower!

Forest rangers also work to prevent intense fires from destroying communities by letting smaller fires burn naturally. Fires are natural events in many forests and grasslands. They help clear away old plant matter, making a fresh start for healthy new plants. If we don't allow smaller fires to happen, the old, dry brush and debris sticks around. This creates a big pile of fuel that could create a really intense fire in the future.

Weather IRL

Many parts of California have hot, dry climates, meaning that wildfires happen quite frequently. In 2018, one of the worst wildfires in the state's history, called the Camp Fire, hit the town of Paradise.

The fire was sparked by a faulty electrical line and burned for almost two entire weeks. It also spread quickly, burning through the area of 80 football fields every minute. Because the fire was so big and so fast, it was able to engulf almost the entire town of Paradise in just about 4 hours. After the fire was finally extinguished, 85 people had died, and an area the size of the city of Chicago had burned.

Why was this fire so big, so fast, and so devastating? Unfortunately, everything in the environment around Paradise that day had created the perfect recipe for wildfire. The area had received much less rain than average, there was plenty of dry vegetation nearby to fuel the fire, and strong winds—up to 70 miles per hour—were fanning the flames.

Rebuilding after a major fire is not easy. In all, the Camp Fire destroyed about 11,000 homes in and near Paradise. A year later, only 11 homes had been rebuilt. There was very little housing available after the fire, and about 90 percent of the population moved out of town—many even moved to different states.

Take Control/Get Involved!

Wildfires can be scary and dangerous, but we can learn all about them in safety using a few simple experiments. In these exercises, you'll learn about the effect of wind on fires, how a firefighter might find the source of a wildfire, and how to plant a fire-safe garden. Grab a grown-up lab partner and your materials, and let's dig in!

1. Wildfire Behavior

Quick Query

The Big Idea: How do wildfires travel uphill—and why do winds make them worse, rather than blowing them out? In this experiment, you'll tip a candle in the angle of a hill and gently blow on the candle to understand these phenomena. What do you think will happen when you blow gently on the flame?

CAUTIONS: Always have a grown-up lab partner present when using matches and candles. Beware of hot wax from the candle, as it can burn you.

Materials:

- Candle
- Matches

The Steps:

1. Have your grown-up lab partner use a match to light the candle.

2. Hold the candle at a slight (small) angle and gently blow on the flame—softly, and not so hard that you blow it out.

3. Observe how the flame changes when you blow on it.

Observations: How did the shape of the flame change when you gently blew on it? Did the flame seem to get stronger or weaker?

Kick It Up a Notch: Increase the angle that the candle is tilted and gently blow on the flame again. How does the shape of the flame when you blow on it change when the candle is held at different angles?

The Hows and Whys: Fires need oxygen to burn, and wind adds oxygen to a fire and causes it to burn faster. The same thing happens when you gently blow air on the candle flame. When you hold the candle at an angle, you should see the flame continue to go up—no matter which way the candle is turned. In nature, wildfires burn uphill much faster than they burn downhill. This is because the fire "preheats" the land that is directly uphill, making it easier to ignite.

2. Follow the Fire

The Big Idea: In nature, wildfire smoke can travel thousands of miles—affecting air quality across entire continents. Satellites track the smoke that moves with the dozens of wind patterns that travel through the atmosphere. In this experiment, a scented candle will fill in for the wildfire, and your nose will act as the satellite. You'll come in from outside and try to find where your grown-up lab partner lit a scented candle. Then you'll map where the scent traveled throughout the house. What factors do you think affected the path that the smoke and scent traveled?

  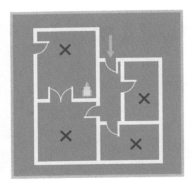

CAUTIONS: Always have a grown-up lab partner present when using matches and candles. Beware of hot wax from the candle, as it can burn you.

Materials:

- Matches
- Scented candle
- Paper
- Pen or pencil

The Steps:

1. Close or blindfold your eyes (or wait outside) while your grown-up lab partner uses a match to light the scented candle and put it in a safe place in another room.

2. Open your eyes, remove the blindfold, or come inside, and use your nose to find the candle.

3. Observe and map in what rooms and locations you can smell the scent of the candle.

Observations: What rooms and locations have the scent of the candle? How long did it take you to find the source of the scent?

Kick It Up a Notch: Try the experiment again, but have your grown-up lab partner light two different candles with two different scents. See if you can still track down the sources!

The Hows and Whys: In real life, scientists often use helicopters or satellites to spot wildfires. They look where the smoke is the densest to find the source of the fire. In this activity, you used the same technique, following the strongest scent to the source of the candle flame.

3. Flowers to Prevent a Fire

Take It Outside!

The Big Idea: Although you can't stop the winds that cause wildfires to spread, you can help make your home safer from wildfires. In this experiment, you'll plan a fire-safe flower bed and garden that will surround a house. Aside from choosing the right plants, what could you do to make a garden safer from fires?

Here are a few fire-safe plants you can include in your garden:

- Moss phlox
- Nanny berry
- Columbine

- Bear berry
- Wintergreen
- Wild geranium

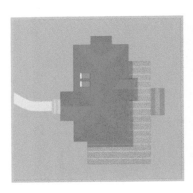  

CAUTIONS: None! This activity is safe for all ages.

Materials:
- Paper
- Pen or pencil

The Steps:

1. Use the paper and pen or pencil to draw a bird's-eye view of a house or apartment building.

2. Draw flower beds with fire-safe plants and other fire-resistant features surrounding the house or apartment building. Try to make the features something that people living in the building would enjoy—while also keeping the building safe from fires.

Observations: What did you take into consideration when designing the garden? Was it easier or more difficult than you expected?

Kick It Up a Notch: Visit some local gardens in your town. Do you see any that appear to be fire safe? Do you see any that seem to need work when it comes to fire safety? If you notice anything in your own gardens that could be improved, talk to your parents about what changes you would make and why.

The Hows and Whys: As people moved into the wilderness to build neighborhoods and houses, they brought with them the plants and flowers they remembered from the places they used to live. Having plants you like isn't a problem, but bringing in plants that aren't native to a region can be. In general, hot, dry climates can only support certain kinds of plants. If you bring in non-native species, they may dry out quickly, creating a fire hazard.

CHAPTER 12

Ice Storms

You look out the window on a cold, gray day. You notice that there is precipitation, but it's not quite snow and not quite rain. After a little while, it appears that your window is coated in a thin layer of crystal-clear ice. Have you ever experienced this phenomenon? If so, you've probably just seen an ice storm!

An **ice storm** refers to the weather conditions that result in about a quarter-inch of ice—or more—accumulating on the ground, houses, cars, and anything else outside in the area of the storm. With the right atmospheric conditions, ice storms can happen almost anywhere. However, in the United States they are most common in the Northeast.

Although a quarter-inch of ice may not seem like much of a natural disaster, this small amount can cause a lot of damage. Even a light layer of ice can cause car accidents on slippery streets. If there's a bit more, the weight of these layers of ice can make electrical lines fall down, causing widespread power outages.

HOW DOES IT DO THAT?

An ice storm is a kind of strange mixture of a snowstorm and a rain shower. As with all precipitation, ice storms start when warm water vapor in the air rises high into the atmosphere, forming a cloud.

However, what happens next is a little bit more complicated. Instead of the water in the cloud falling as rain or snow, it sort of falls as both. Here's how it works: An ice-storm cloud is made of ice crystals, just like any other snow cloud. As the tiny ice crystals begin to clump together, they get heavier, falling out of the cloud as snowflakes. As the snow falls, it passes through a layer of warm air. This warmer part of the atmosphere causes the snowflake to melt into rain. As the newly-formed raindrop continues to fall, it encounters a below-freezing layer of air near the ground.

If the rain freezes in the air before it hits the ground, it becomes sleet—a chunky mixture of ice and rain. However, if the rain doesn't freeze in the air, the water becomes **supercooled**. This means that, even though it's below freezing temperature, the water is still a liquid, but it becomes frozen ice as soon as it comes into contact with a surface. This is freezing rain, and that is what causes an ice storm.

Freezing rain can make the environment look beautiful. When everything is covered with a layer of ice, it looks like a glittering winter wonderland! But don't be fooled: An ice storm can be very dangerous. Even a layer of ice only a tenth of an inch thick can make roads feel like skating rinks, causing cars to slide past stop signs or right off the road. As thicker layers of ice begin to accumulate, the weight of the ice becomes substantial.

The heavy layers of ice can cause tree branches to become 30 percent heavier and add up to 500 pounds of weight to power lines—made even worse by gusty winds. This can cause tree branches to break off and fall onto houses and into streets. Power lines can become so heavy that lines snap, causing widespread power outages.

Power outages can be dangerous at any time of year, but they can be especially devastating in the winter. It can take days or weeks to repair all the lines and bring power back to a community. In subzero temperatures, people who lose electricity may have no other way to heat their homes—leading to dangerously cold temperatures even indoors.

Pop Culture Quiz!

In Disney's movie *Frozen*, Princess Elsa has a superpower: She can create ice and snow whenever and wherever she wants. She can use her powers to play—like to build a snowman. At one point in the movie, she even builds a giant ice castle to live in.

Now, I think we all know that this movie isn't exactly based on fact, but let's see how Elsa's powers in *Frozen* stack up to a real ice storm with this short movie quiz!

True or False: Ice storms are caused by people with magical powers who can shoot icy wind out of their hands.

False! (I hope this one was pretty easy.) In real life, there is no person who can control weather events—including ice storms—on demand. So what really causes an ice storm? Ice storms are generally caused by freezing rain. This happens naturally, based on conditions in the atmosphere—no magical powers required!

True or False: When Princess Anna meets Olaf the snowman for the first time in an icy forest, they are surrounded by ice-covered branches hanging down from trees. This can happen in real life, too.

True! When an ice storm rolls through town, freezing rain covers almost every surface—including tree branches—in a clear glaze of ice. The trees in the forest in *Frozen* have droopy branches, much like a weeping willow tree. Check out how the movie compares to these pictures of ice covered branches in real life.

One of the worst ice storms in US history happened in parts of New England, New York, and southern Canada in January 1998. Why was this storm so devastating? The ice from this storm accumulated to three inches thick, causing lots of damage—including power outages for millions of people in the region. Icy streets, as well as fallen branches and power lines, made transportation extremely difficult.

Fixing all of the damage caused by this ice storm cost billions of dollars. And in the United States and Canada combined, the ice storm caused more than 40 people to die, while over 1,000 more were injured.

It took crews several weeks to repair power lines and restore electricity to the communities hit hardest by the storm. However, the damage to the nearby forests took much longer to repair. The ice storm killed or severely damaged up to 20 percent of the trees in the region, and many more had light to moderate damage.

As Earth's climate changes, evidence suggests that extreme weather will become more commonplace than ever. Devastating ice storms may become more frequent in parts of the United States and Canada as the planet warms.

Take Control/Get Involved!

What's the best way to de-ice a sidewalk? How does ice bring down a power line? Can rain really freeze in the air? Answer these questions and more with the experiments that are up next!

1. Icy Sidewalk

Quick Query

The Big Idea: In an ice storm, sidewalks and roads are covered with ice and are unsafe for driving and walking. Cities and towns usually use salt to help melt the ice, but is that the best choice we have? In this experiment, you'll try a variety of substances to test what works best in an ice storm.

CAUTIONS: Clean up any water from melting ice immediately so that you don't slip.

Materials:

- Ice cubes
- Rimmed baking pan or plastic box
- Salt
- Clock, stopwatch, or timer app on a smartphone or tablet
- Pen or pencil
- Sugar
- Beet juice
- Pickle juice

continued →

The Steps:

1. Place the ice cubes in the rimmed baking pan or plastic box.

2. Sprinkle the salt over the ice cubes.

3. Using the clock, stopwatch, or timer app, time how long it takes for half of the ice to melt. Record the time on the table that follows using the pen or pencil.

4. Repeat steps 1 to 3 using sugar, beet juice, and pickle juice in place of salt. Then repeat them using a mixture of beet juice and salt.

Observations: Did the salt, sugar, beet juice, pickle juice, or salty beet juice cause the ice to melt fastest?

Kick It Up a Notch: What other substances could you use to melt ice? Try them out.

The Hows and Whys: Salt has been used to de-ice roads and sidewalks for decades. Why does it work? Salt lowers the melting temperature of ice. This means that even if it's still freezing outside, you can sprinkle salt on the sidewalk and melt the ice. Pickle juice also has salt in it, so it may have the same effect. What about the other substances? Sugar probably won't have much effect, nor will beet juice on its own. But beet juice mixed with salt will make a sticky mixture that melts the ice all over. This is a formula sometimes used on roads.

SUBSTANCE	TIME FOR HALF OF ICE TO MELT
Salt	
Sugar	
Beet juice	
Pickle juice	
Salty beet juice	

2. Weighty Ice

Observation Deck

The Big Idea: Ice storms can be dangerous for many reasons, including downed power lines. Here, you'll learn why ice storms bring down power lines while rain does not. How many ice cubes do you think you would need to weigh down your model power line?

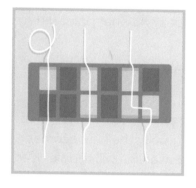  

CAUTIONS: Have a grown-up lab partner poke holes in the shoe box.

Materials:

- 3 pieces of string or shoelaces
- Ice-cube tray
- Water
- Shoe box
- Chopsticks

The Steps:

1. Place one of the strings/shoelaces in the ice-cube tray so that its center is in one ice-cube compartment. Fill that one compartment with water. Place the second string/shoelace so that its center is in two ice-cube compartments, and fill those two compartments with water. Place the third string/shoelace so that its center is in three ice-cube compart-ments, and pour water into those three compartments.

2. Place the ice-cube tray with the strings in it in the freezer until the water freezes and forms ice cubes.

3. While the water is freezing in the ice-cube trays, set the shoe box upside down and poke holes in the bottom. These will hold your "poles" (chopsticks).

continued →

4. When the ice cubes on the strings are frozen, start with the one-ice-cube string and attach an end of the string to each chopstick. Put the other end of each chopstick into a hole in the box.

5. See which string of ice cubes (one ice cube, two ice cubes, or three ice cubes) is needed to weigh down the chopsticks and string.

Observations: What happened as you added more ice cubes? At what point did the chopsticks fall over?

Kick It Up a Notch: Design a better power line. What design would you use to keep the power line from sagging in an ice storm?

The Hows and Whys: Ice weighs much more than water, so an ice storm does much more damage to power lines and trees than rainwater. Eventually, the ice becomes so heavy that the line will snap, or the poles that hold the power line will topple over.

3. Frozen Bubbles

Take It Outside

The Big Idea: Ice doesn't need to fall out of the sky to be dangerous. On very cold days, even a small amount of rain can create an instantaneous slippery ice mat. In this experiment, you'll see just how quickly ice can freeze in the form of a bubble. What do you think will happen if the bubble freezes before it reaches the ground?

CAUTIONS: Always wear cold-weather clothing when going outside on below-freezing days!

Note: I know that not everyone lives in a climate where days get this cold in the winter. Unfortunately, this experiment won't work at higher temperatures. If you have this problem, and you know someone who lives in a cold enough climate, maybe they can do the experiment with you over video chat.

Materials:

- Very cold weather, such as 10°F (−23°C) or colder
- Bubble liquid
- Bubble wand

The Steps:

1. Dress appropriately to be outside in temperatures below freezing. Take the bubble liquid and wand outside.

2. Dip the bubble wand in the bubble liquid and blow a bubble. Blow the bubble up into the air.

3. Observe whether the bubble freezes and what happens to it when it reaches the ground.

continued →

Observations: Did the bubble freeze? Why or why not? What happens when a frozen bubble reaches the ground?

Kick It Up a Notch: What happens if you blow bubbles of different sizes? How long does it take different-size bubbles to freeze? What happens when the bubbles fall to the ground from different heights?

The Hows and Whys: Freezing rain is caused by water droplets that fall and become supercooled in a cold layer of air near the ground—eventually freezing on a surface. In this experiment, the bubble works a bit like freezing rain—freezing in the cold air just above the ground.

CHAPTER 13

Weather or Not?

Now that you've learned about all of the wild weather that we can experience on Earth, you might be wondering: What is the *most* dangerous weather on Earth?

Read on to find out!

In the United States in 2018, 782 people died in weather-related events, and 1,797 were injured. Hurricanes and tornadoes certainly cause a lot of damage each year, but they aren't always the most dangerous to human life. For example, the weather events that caused the most death and injury in the United States in 2018 were heat and winter weather.

That same year, the United States experienced 14 separate weather disasters that each caused more than a billion dollars' worth of damage, including droughts, tornadoes, hurricanes, hailstorms, and more.

Unfortunately, expensive disasters are becoming more frequent. The number of disasters—and the cost of their damage—has been going up in recent years. Why? The answers are complicated, but Earth's changing climate is one reason. Climate change is leading to more frequent extreme weather events—and more extreme repair costs.

As our climate changes—and our weather changes along with it—it is important to understand what's going on in our atmosphere. In this book, we've explained the basics of the weather we see and hear about every day. But there's so much more we need to know to prepare for future weather events.

Fortunately, meteorologists and other scientists are on the case. They use information from Doppler radar, satellites, weather stations, weather balloons, and computer models to learn more about the conditions in the atmosphere that lead to major weather events.

What exactly are they working on? Well, one major goal is improving weather forecasting. Right now, we can predict the weather a few days from now fairly accurately. This is helpful when you're trying to plan outdoor activities. But more time would give us a better chance to prepare for severe weather—by evacuating or sheltering in place, for example.

Earth's climate is changing due to global warming, and we know that human activities are contributing to the change. Scientists agree on this. But climate is on such a long time scale. Why do we care if Earth is a degree or two warmer today than it was when our great-grandparents were born?

It actually matters quite a lot! Even though the difference between 73 degrees and 74 degrees on a warm spring day may not seem like much, when it comes to the average temperature over the whole globe, a small change is a big deal.

For example, as Earth warms—even a small amount—extreme weather events will become more frequent. Between 1980 and 2014, the number of catastrophic weather events around the world tripled from almost 300 per year to more than 900. So meteorologists and other scientists are working on improving warning systems, which can save lives.

As the climate changes, hot regions on Earth will only become hotter. By understanding which regions will experience the biggest temperature increases, scientists can help local officials and medical workers prepare for changing needs. For example, warmer temperatures will require more water and more healthcare workers who are trained to treat heat-related health conditions.

Another result of climate change is rising sea levels. As Earth warms, glaciers are melting, leading to more water in the oceans. This, along with a few other factors, results in higher sea levels. In fact, over the past 100 years, sea levels have risen about seven inches.

This is a major problem for coastal communities. When big storms bring massive waves, higher sea levels mean more damage. So Earth scientists are using many tools to track sea-level change and the factors that influence it.

Now, you probably don't have access to a satellite, a Doppler radar, or a research airplane. Although these are the tools that meteorologists and other scientists use to study the atmosphere, you can learn a great deal about how weather forms using much simpler equipment at home.

For example, in this book we've done experiments to learn about

- cloud formation

- changes in air pressure

- the water cycle

- what particles travel farthest in a dust storm

- how a thunderstorm forms

Although the scale is different—real clouds are much, much bigger than a pickle jar, for example—the science behind the experiments is the same as what's happening in our atmosphere.

We hope that the next time you see a rain cloud or feel the wind on your face, you'll think about the experiments you performed as you followed me through this book. As we went from chapter 1 to chapter 13, we hope you gained confidence, and your "why?" questions have now become exclamations of, "I know why!"

Understanding how our atmosphere works to create the weather we experience every day is no easy task. We know you won't understand it all even after reading this book and following along with the experiments, but we hope this will be a jumping-off point for your own curiosity. Maybe you'll ask some new questions and answer them by designing your own experiments!

Whether you decide to become a meteorologist or an artist or a chef when you grow up, the weather will always be a part of your life. And now you'll know a lot more about why things are the way they are.

Thank you for learning with me, and I hope you enjoy the rest of your journey into the world of weather!

Glossary

advection fog: A type of fog that forms when warm air meets a cool surface

aerosols: Tiny particles such as smoke, pollen, and dust that float around in the atmosphere

air pressure: The weight of the molecules in the air pushing down on Earth's surface

atmosphere: The layers of gases and particles that surround Earth

avalanche: A mass of snow that slides down a mountain

barometer: An instrument used to detect local changes in air pressure

climate: The average weather conditions in a region over decades, centuries, or even longer

climate change: A significant change in the average weather conditions—temperature, rainfall, etc.—in a place over decades, centuries, or more

cold front: The changeover region where a mass of cold air moves toward, and then slides underneath, a mass of warm air, thrusting the warm air higher in the atmosphere

condensation: The process by which a gas turns into a liquid

Coriolis effect: An interaction between the atmosphere and Earth's rotation on its axis, causing winds in the Northern Hemisphere to bend toward the right, and the winds in the Southern Hemisphere to bend toward the left

crown fire: A wildfire that burns the leaves and branches in the tops of trees or bushes

Doldrums: A region of the ocean near the equator that has very calm winds, leaving many sailing ships stranded

downdraft: An air current that moves downward in the atmosphere as cold air sinks

drought: An event that occurs when a region gets much less rain than usual over a long period of time, often leading to decreased water supply

dust storm: An event that occurs when winds are so strong that they pick up and blow particles of soil into the atmosphere, eventually dropping the soil particles somewhere else

evaporation: The process by which a liquid turns into a gas

flash flood: An event with heavy rain when waters rise so fast that buildings can flood and people can get caught off guard; common in urban areas with many paved surfaces

glacier: A natural ice formation made up of snow that piles up over many years, with each new layer of snow pressing down on the layer beneath it

global warming: An increase in the average temperature of Earth's surface, oceans, and atmosphere caused by increased amounts of greenhouse gases in the atmosphere

greenhouse effect: The process by which gases in Earth's atmosphere trap some of the Sun's heat, causing the planet to be warmer

greenhouse gases: Heat-trapping gases in the atmosphere, including water vapor, carbon dioxide, and methane

ground fire: A wildfire that burns under the ground, using roots and other underground organic material as fuel

humidity: The amount of water vapor in the air

hurricane: A spinning storm with fast winds that happens above warm waters in the North Atlantic Ocean or eastern Pacific Ocean

hypothesis: In a scientific experiment, a hypothesis is a testable idea about why something happens the way it does

ice fog: A type of fog that occurs in extremely cold air temperatures when water vapor freezes into small ice crystals instead of condensing into water droplets

ice storm: The weather conditions that result in about a quarter inch of ice—or more—accumulating on the ground, houses, cars, and anything else outside in the area

jet stream: A band of extremely fast-moving wind high up in the atmosphere

meteorology: The field of science that involves studying our atmosphere, how it changes, and how it affects our weather

monsoon: An extreme rain that happens in India and nearby regions when the Sun heats the ocean and the land unevenly

natural disaster: A terrible event in nature that results in serious damage to property—including houses, roads, or even entire cities—and often in many deaths, completely changing the lives of people who live nearby

precipitation: The result of water vapor in the atmosphere condensing and falling from the clouds, such as rain or snow

radiation fog: A type of fog that forms when moist air approaches the cool ground, causing condensation (the formation of water droplets) in the air—just like a cloud

scientific method: The organized process that scientists use to answer questions about the natural world and how it works

snow cornice: A formation that occurs when snow is blown by the wind at the sharp edge of a ridge or cliff face, creating a ledge of snow and ice

snow penitents: Spikes of snow that become compacted by certain melting and evaporation patterns

steam fog: A type of fog that forms over the tops of lakes, usually in the fall and winter seasons

supercell: An unusually large, rotating thunderstorm

supercooling: A phenomenon that happens when water is below freezing but remains a liquid—turning into solid ice when it comes into contact with a surface

surface fire: A wildfire that burns grasses, brush, or other vegetation on top of Earth's surface

tornado: A spinning tube of air that extends from a thunderstorm cloud in the sky all the way down to the ground

trade winds: Winds that blow steadily from east to west in a curved pattern toward the equator

tropical cyclone: A spinning storm with fast winds that happens above warm waters in the South Atlantic Ocean or Indian Ocean

typhoon: A spinning storm with fast winds that happens above warm waters in the western Pacific Ocean

updraft: An air current that moves upward in the atmosphere as warm air rises

valley fog: A type of fog that forms in mountainous areas, usually at night, filling the valleys between mountains

warm front: The changeover region where a warm air mass is replacing a cold air mass in the atmosphere

water cycle: The movement of water on Earth from the soil and oceans to clouds, then to precipitation, then back to the soil and oceans

water vapor: The gas form of water

weather: A description of the conditions in Earth's atmosphere at a certain place and time

weather phenomenon: A weather event, whether it is as routine as a light rainstorm or as extreme as a hurricane

weather satellite: A machine that orbits high above Earth, collecting information about the temperature, gases, water vapor, and clouds in our atmosphere

weather station: A setup of several different types of instruments that constantly collect information about the weather in a specific area

wildfire: An uncontrolled fire that is fueled by vegetation such as plants and trees

wind: Air movement caused by differences in air temperature and pressure

Resources

National Geographic

nationalgeographic.com

National Geographic has a ton of great reference pages about the weather phenomena we discussed in this book and many more, including the latest news.

Weather Wiz Kids

weatherwizkids.com

Designed by a meteorologist, Weather Wiz Kids is a good resource for kid-friendly information about weather, as well as more experiments you can do to explore weather concepts indoors and out.

Space Weather Center

spaceweathercenter.org

Did you know that Earth also experiences weather from the Sun? This weather is called space weather, and if it's extreme, it can cause all kind of problems here on Earth, such as power outages. Check out this page to learn more!

PBS LearningMedia: Earth and Space Science

pbslearningmedia.org/subjects/science/earth-and-space-science/weather-and-climate

Want to suggest some cool weather and climate lessons for your teachers and classmates? Take a look at the lessons and activities offered by PBS LearningMedia.

Weather for Kids

weatherforkids.org

Check out this website for more information about the weather phenomena you read about in this book, as well as many others. You'll also be able to try a weather quiz when you feel like you've become a weather master!

DK Find Out: Weather

dkfindout.com/us/earth/weather/

This website has some great explanations of everyday and extreme weather events. If you learn better from visual explanations, this website has some awesome diagrams that draw out exactly how things work.

Smithsonian Weather Lab

ssec.si.edu/weather-lab

Meteorologists create models to predict what will happen next in our weather. You can use the Smithsonian Weather Lab to learn to make these predictions, too! While you're there, you can check out their weather games as well.

National Severe Storms Laboratory: Severe Weather 101

nssl.noaa.gov/education/svrwx101

Want to learn more about severe weather such as tornadoes and hurricanes? Check out the articles and latest research here!

National Weather Service: JetStream—An Online School for Weather

weather.gov/jetstream/

The National Weather Service, which is responsible for monitoring and forecasting the weather in the United States, offers a great online "weather school" with everything you could ever want to know about the weather that affects our lives. Check it out if you want to take a deep dive into what makes our atmosphere tick!

National Geographic Kids: *Everything Weather* by Kathy Furgang (book)

If you want to load up on weather facts to stump your family and friends, this book is a great place to start! There are also lots of amazing photographs that will really spark wonder.

National Geographic Kids: Climate Change

kids.nationalgeographic.com/explore/science/climate-change

Want to learn more about how Earth's climate is changing—and what that could mean for our weather in the near future? This page is a great introduction to the effects of Earth's warming climate.

Experiment Index

Chapter 3
Up in Smoke! 18
Pressure's On: Make Your
   Own Barometer 20
Particle Catchers 22

Chapter 4
Clouds in the Kitchen 33
Staying Cool Under a Cloud 35
Cloud Journaling 38

Chapter 5
Soil Soaker 48
Water Cycle in a Bag 50
Rain Tracker 52

Chapter 6
Frost in a Can 60
Snowflake Factory 62
How Much Water Is in Snow? 64

Chapter 7
Fog in a Jar 71
Smog in a Jar 73
Seeing Through the Fog 75

Chapter 8
Tabletop Dust Storm 83
Dust Storm vs. Sandstorm 85
Mapping Dust Storms 87

Chapter 9
Doppler Effect 97
How Does a Storm Form? 99
Keep the Outside from Getting In 101

Chapter 10
Wind Spinner 109
The Big Wave 111
Track a Hurricane 113

Chapter 11
Wildfire Behavior 122
Follow the Fire 124
Flowers to Prevent a Fire 126

Chapter 12
Icy Sidewalk 133
Weighty Ice 135
Frozen Bubbles 137

Index

A

advection fog, 68, 145
aerosols, 17, 145
  dust storms, 80
  Particle Catcher (experiment), 22–23
air pressure, 9, 145
  barometer, 17
  Pressure's On: Make Your Own
    Barometer (experiment), 20–21
altocumulus clouds, 27, 30
altostratus clouds, 27, 30
Andes Mountains, snow penitents, 58
anemometers, 109
Antarctica, 15, 59, 117
atmosphere, 7, 145
avalanche, 57, 145

B

balloons, 14, 142
barometer, 145
  air pressure measurement, 17
  experiment for making, 20–21
The Big Wave (experiment), 111–112
black blizzards, 81
Bodélé Depression, 82

C

California
  Camp Fire in 2018, 120
  fire season, 118
  wind energy, 16
campfires, 118, 120
cirrocumulus clouds, 26, 30
cirrostratus clouds, 27, 30
cirrus clouds, 26, 30
climate, vi, 145
  description of, 8
  weather or, 119

climate change, ix, 10, 142–143, 145
  description of, 10
  flooding and, 47
Cloud Journaling (experiment), 38–40
clouds, 25
  altocumulus, 27
  altostratus, 27
  Atacama Desert in South America, 32
  cirrocumulus, 26
  cirrostratus, 27
  cirrus, 26
  Cloud Journaling (experiment), 38–40
  Clouds in the Kitchen
    (experiment), 33–34
  cumulonimbus, 28, 29
  cumulus, 28
  experiments, 32, 33–40
  Faroe Islands, 32
  high (16,000 to 43,000 ft.), 26–27
  lenticular, 29
  low (surface to 7,000 ft.), 28–29
  mid-level (7,000 to 23,000 ft.), 27
  nimbostratus, 28
  Staying Cool Under a Cloud
    (experiment), 35–37
  stratus, 28
  unusual, 29
Clouds in the Kitchen
  (experiment), 33–34
cold front, 31, 145
condensation, 30, 31, 145
condenses, water vapor, 25
Coriolis effect, 15, 106, 145
crown fire, 118, 145
cumulonimbus clouds, 28, 29, 30, 31
cumulus clouds, 28, 30, 31

D

DK Find Out, 149
Doldrums, 13, 145
Doppler Effect (experiment), 97–98
Doppler radar, 97, 98, 142, 143
downdraft, 84, 94, 145
drought, 45, 91, 145
dry snow, 56
Dust Bowl, 81
dust storm, 145
  description of, 79
  Dust Storm vs. Sandstorm
    (experiment), 85–86
  experiments, 82, 83–88
  extremes, 82
  formation of, 80–81
  landscapes and, 81
  Mapping Dust Storms
    (experiment), 87–88
  photos of, 81
  Tabletop Dust Storm
    (experiment), 83–84
  updrafts, 80
Dust Storm vs. Sandstorm
  (experiment), 85–86

E

Earth's atmosphere, weather
  and climate, 9
Earth's rotation, hurricane and, 106
energy, wind, 16
Enhanced Fujita (EF) scale, 95
evaporation, 30, 31, 145
experiments, vii
  The Big Wave, 111–112
  Cloud Journaling, 38–40
  Clouds in the Kitchen, 33–34
  Doppler Effect, 97–98
  Dust Storm vs. Sandstorm, 85–86
  Flowers to Prevent a Fire, 126–127
  Fog in a Jar, 71–72

Follow the Fire, 124–125
Frost in a Can, 60–61
Frozen Bubbles, 137–138
How Does a Storm Form?, 99–100
How Much Water is in Snow?, 64–65
Icy Sidewalk, 133–134
Keep the Outside From
  Getting In, 101–102
Pressure's On: Make Your
  Own Barometer, 20–21
Mapping Dust Storms, 87–88
Particle Catchers, 22–23
Rain Tracker, 52–53
scientific method, viii
Seeing Through the Fog, 75–76
Smog in a Jar, 73–74
Snowflake Factory, 62–63
Soil Soaker, 48–49
Staying Cool Under a Cloud, 35–37
Tabletop Dust Storm, 83–84
Track a Hurricane, 113–114
Up in Smoke (experiment), 18–19
Water Cycle in a Bag, 50–51
Weighty Ice, 135–136
Wildfire Behavior, 122–123
Wind Spinner, 109–110
eye, hurricane, 107

F

Faroe Islands, 32
fire. See wildfire
fireworks, 118, 120
flash flood, 45, 146
floods, 91
Florida
  hurricane, 106, 107
  tornado, 96
  typical weather days, 7
  weather change, 9
Flowers to Prevent a Fire
  (experiment), 126–127

fog
    advection fog, 68
    experiments, 69, 70–76
    extremes, 68
    Fog in a Jar (experiment), 71–72
    formation, 68
    ice fog, 69
    phenomenon in horror movies, 70
    radiation fog, 68
    Seeing Through the Fog
        (experiment), 75–76
    Smog in a Jar (experiment), 73–74
    steam fog, 69
    valley fog, 69
    weather phenomenon, 67–69
Fog in a Jar (experiment), 71–72
follow the fire (experiment), 124–125
forest rangers, 120
Frost in a Can (experiment), 60–61
Frozen Bubbles (experiment), 137–138

G

glacier, 57, 143, 146
global warming, 10, 146
glossary, 145–148
Grand Banks, Newfoundland, fog, 68
Great Plains
    Tornado Alley, 93
    wind, 16
greenhouse effect, 10, 146
greenhouse gases, 10, 146
ground fire, 118, 146
Guam, 59

H

How Does a Storm Form?
    (experiment), 99–100
How Much Water is in Snow?
    (experiment), 64–65
humidity, 44, 146

hurricane, 91, 146
    Atlantic hurricane season 2017, 107
    The Big Wave (experiment), 111–112
    Coriolis effect, 106
    description of, 105
    experiments, 108, 109–114
    eye of, 107
    formation of, 106–107
    rain bands, 107
    storm surge, 108
    Track a Hurricane
        (experiment), 113–114
    tropical cyclone, 106
    typhoon, 106
    Wind Spinner (experiment), 109–110
Hurricane Harvey, 107
Hurricane Irma, 91, 107
Hurricane Maria, 107
Hurricane Nate, 107
Hurricane Sandy, 91
hurricane season, 91, 105, 107
hypothesis, viii, 146
    scientific method, viii, 2–3

I

ice fog, 69, 146
ice storm, 146
    description of, 129
    experiments, 132, 133–138
    formation of, 130, 132
    Frozen Bubbles (experiment),
        137–138
    Icy Sidewalk (experiment), 133–134
    northeast US and Canada
        1998 storm, 132
    pop culture quiz, 131
    Weighty Ice (experiment), 135–136
Icy Sidewalk (experiment), 133–134
infiltration, 31

J

Japanese Alps, snow, 59
jet stream, 15–16, 146, 150
journaling, cloud, 38–40

K

Kansas, wind energy, 16
Keep the Outside From Getting
    In (experiment), 101–102

L

lenticular clouds, 29, 30
life skills, ix

M

Mapping Dust Storms
    (experiment), 87–88
Mawsynram, India, rainfall, 46
meteorologists
    clouds, 39
    friendly neighborhood, 8–9
    predicting disastrous phenomenon, 91
    rain gauge, 53
    tornadoes, 94
meteorology, 8, 146
Michigan, typical weather days, 7
monsoon, 46, 146

N

National Geographic, 149
National Geographic Kids, 150
National Severe Storms Laboratory, 150
National Weather Service, 150
natural disaster, 7, 91, 146
nimbostratus clouds, 28, 30

O

Oklahoma
    dust storm, 81
    tornado, 93
    wind energy, 16

P

Particle Catchers (experiment), 22–23
PBS Learning Media, 149
phenomenon, vii. See also
    weather phenomenon
Phoenix, Arizona, dust storm, 81
Pixar, 14
pop culture quiz, 95, 131
precipitation, 31, 43, 147. See also rain
Pressure's On: Make Your Own
    Barometer (experiment), 20–21

Q

quiz, pop culture, 95, 131

R

radiation fog, 68, 147
rain. See also ice storm
    description, 43
    droughts, 45
    experiments, 47, 48–53
    extremes, 46
    flash flood, 45
    freezing, 130
    monsoon, 46
    precipitation, 43
    Rain Tracker (experiment), 52–53
    Soil Soaker (experiment), 48–49
    water cycle, 44–45
    Water Cycle in a Bag
        (experiment), 50–51
rain clouds, 30–31, 143
Rain Tracker (experiment), 52–53
research airplanes, 8, 143
resources, 149–150

S

Sahara Desert, dust storm, 81
satellite, 142, 143
    clouds, 39
    dust storm, 81, 87, 88

satellite (continued)
  hurricane, 114
  weather, 8, 148
  wildfire, 124, 125
science, vi–vii
scientific method, 2, 147
  experiments, viii
  hypothesis, 2–3
  testing ideas, 3–4
sea levels, 143
Seattle, rainfall, 46
Seeing Through the Fog
    (experiment), 75–76
Smithsonian Weather Lab, 150
smog, 73
Smog in a Jar (experiment), 73–74
snow
  avalanches, 57
  climate and, 55
  dry snow, 56
  experiments, 59, 60–65
  extremes, 59
  formation of, 56
  Frost in a Can (experiment), 60–61
  glaciers, 57
  How Much Water is in Snow?
      (experiment), 64–65
  snow cornice, 57, 58
  Snowflake Factory
      (experiment), 62–63
  snow penitents, 58
  wet snow, 56
snow cornice, 147
Snowflake Factory (experiment), 62–63
snowman snow, 56
snow penitents, 58, 147
Soil Soaker (experiment), 48–49
South America, cloud-free
    Atacama Desert, 32
Space Weather Center, 149

Staying Cool Under a Cloud
    (experiment), 35–37
steam fog, 69, 147
storm chasers, tornados, 95
storm surge, 108, 111–112
stratus clouds, 28, 30
supercell, 94, 98, 147
supercooled, 130
supercooling, 147
surface fire, 118, 147

T

Tabletop Dust Storm
    (experiment), 83–84
Texas, wind energy, 16
thunderstorms, vi
  clouds, 27
  dust storm, 80, 81
  hurricanes, 105–107
  rain, 45
  tornadoes, 93–95
  winds, 80
tornado, 147
  description of, 93
  Doppler effect (experiment), 97–98
  Enhanced Fujita scale, 95
  experiments, 96, 97–102
  formation of, 94–95
  How Does a Storm Form?
      (experiment), 99–100
  Keep the Outside From Getting
      In (experiment), 101–102
  March 3, 2019 event in
      southeastern US, 96
  pop culture quiz, 95
  storm chasers, 95
  supercells, 94, 98
  thunderstorms, 94
Tornado Alley, 93
tornado season, 91, 93
tornado warning, 95

tornado watch, 95
Track a Hurricane (experiment), 113–114
trade winds, 13, 147
transpiration, 31
tropical cyclone, 106, 147
Twister (movie), 95
typhoon, 106, 147

U

United States
  hurricanes, 91, 107
  tornadoes, 93
  wildfires, 120
Up (movie), 14
updraft, 80, 84, 94, 147
Up in Smoke (experiment), 18–19
US Virgin Islands, 59

V

valley fog, 69, 147

W

warm front, 30, 147
water cycle, 44–45, 148
Water Cycle in a Bag (experiment), 50–51
water vapor, 25, 148
weather, vi, 148
  changes in, 142–144
  climate or, 119
  control of, 1
  description of, 8
weather balloons, 14, 142
Weather Facts for Kids, 149
weather phenomena, vii, 148
  clouds, 25, 26–29
  definition of, 7
  dust storms, 79–81
  fog, 67–69
  hurricane, 105, 106–108
  ice storm, 129–132

rain, 44–45, 47
  snow, 55–59
  tornado, 93, 94–95
  wildfire, 117–120
  wind, 13–16
weather satellite, 8, 148
weather skills, ix
weather station, 8, 142, 148
Weather Wiz Kids, 149
Weighty Ice (experiment), 135–136
wet snow, 56
wildfire, 91, 148
  Camp Fire in California 2018, 120
  description of, 117
  experiments, 121, 122–127
  Flowers to Prevent a Fire (experiment), 126–127
  Follow the Fire (experiment), 124–125
  formation of, 118–120
  Wildfire Behavior (experiment), 122–123
  wind and, 119
Wildfire Behavior (experiment), 122–123
wind, 148
  description of, 14–15
  dust storms, 79–81
  experiments, 17, 18–23
  jet streams, 15–16
  Particle Catchers (experiment), 22–23
  Pressure's On: Make Your Own Barometer (experiment), 20–21
  Up in Smoke (experiment), 18–19
  weather phenomenon, 13–16
  wildfire and, 119
wind energy, 16
windmills, 16
wind speed, Antarctica, 15
Wind Spinner (experiment), 109–110
wind turbines, 16
The Wizard of Oz (movie), 93

Acknowledgments

Thank you to the thousands of meteorologists and scientists who work very hard to understand our atmosphere and our changing climate. Severe weather doesn't happen on a 9-to-5 schedule, and I know there are lots of nights, weekends, and summer vacations spent studying, chasing, and explaining storms. I appreciate all you do to help us keep our species and our planet safe!

Thanks also to the science journalists, writers, and educators who work (just as hard) to translate this cutting-edge science for the rest of us. Without either contribution, this book would not have been possible.

And thanks most of all to my brilliantly kind and patient husband, Tim. You cared for our small children all by yourself for many weekends so that I could shut myself in a room and write this book. And you did it all while social distancing during a global pandemic. This was a herculean task, and I'm so grateful that we're on the same team!

About the Author

Jessica Stoller-Conrad is a science writer specializing in content for young audiences. In her most recent role, she produces digital content that explains space and Earth science for kids. Previously, she wrote for a variety of news outlets and institutions covering biology, engineering, health, and food. Jessica holds a master's degree in biological sciences from the University of Notre Dame. She lives with her husband and two sons in Southern California.